From

Wreck

to

Wonderful
Wholeness

From

Wreck

to

Wonderful
Wholeness

Edel Kearney

RESOURCE *Publications* • Eugene, Oregon

FROM WRECK TO WONDERFUL WHOLENESS

Resource Publications
An Imprint of Wipf and Stock Publishers
199 W. 8th Ave., Suite 3
Eugene, OR 97401

www.wipfandstock.com

PAPERBACK ISBN: 978-1-5326-3693-6
HARDCOVER ISBN: 978-1-5326-3695-0
EBOOK ISBN: 978-1-5326-3694-3

Manufactured in the U.S.A.   SEPTEMBER 20, 2017

For Mam

Contents

Introduction

New Life Cover.

Nobody wants to hear another boring story of transformation and a holier than thou story of "seeing the light," yet everyone does want to know how to live happier, healthier, and more meaningful lives. This is only human nature, as we all desire much the same thing, but how we go about it is where we differ. We all take different routes to arrive at our presupposed destination of happiness, contentment, and inner peace. I, for one, was tormented for years, and fell, as so many do, into the pit of alcohol addiction. It took me a long time to crawl out of the hole I had dug for myself, but I did climb out, and I came out stronger and much better for it. But what I learned along the way is not only for those suffering from addiction, but for all who want to empower themselves—that is, anyone who is genuinely interested in honoring and motivating themselves to live a life lived in wholeness, encompassing mind, body, and soul. Mind, body, and soul is the original trinity, still standing today, and it is a formula that will never falter. This, of course, I learned the hard way, but anyone can do it a lot easier. You do not need to be a rip-roaring alcoholic to kickstart a new life plan. All it takes is an intention and a commitment to taking your life, spirituality, health, well-being, and your soul seriously as the soul is who you really are, not who is looking back at you in the mirror. After that, it is not rocket science, just common sense and a willingness to invest time in yourself. View it as a new life insurance policy, the best cover you can get. It even goes beyond the confines of this world and into the next level. No pre-existing insurance company can offer you that. Investment in your personal growth is worth more to you than any material investment plan you can ever make. It will equip and cover you for life. Here in this little book I share with you my story and how I found my route to fulfillment and happiness. This is my journey from wreck to wonderful wholeness. I invested in my personal growth, and already it has paid me generously. Money cannot and would not cover what my life experience and God has taught me. All I have learned has been invaluable to me, and I have a responsibility to share that with people—if they are willing and interested in listening, of course. I hope that if not all of what I have to say interests you, that you can find some elements in the book that will help you in some way. This is a small contribution written by me in gratitude for a life now lived beyond my wildest expectations, and a life which for me is only just beginning.

Chapter 1

Following Your Intuition

One opportunity that came my way was the chance to go to do some work in Lourdes, France. Lourdes, being one of the largest Catholic pilgrimage sites in the world, excited me, and I had never been before, but being fresh out of rehab I hesitated. It was a huge gamble for me to leave my family, my friends, and my AA group, essentially all my support behind me, to spend six months in a foreign country where I knew no one and I did not even speak the language. To cut a long story short, seven years later I am still there and it has become my home. But here is where I found I could discover my true self. A lack of distractions and peace allowed me to deepen and develop my personal growth. The opportunity allowed me to truly discover my inner essence. The environment of the sanctuary, the nature of the town—every shop sold religious goods such as statues of angels, saints, Mother Mary, candles, rosary beads, religious medals, icons—you name it, all was in my face and I loved it. It fed my religious and spiritual fascinations. I felt and was transformed by the feminine energy that Mother Mary brings here. Her presence can be clouded over by the crowds, the noise, and the neon lights, but she is nonetheless here. Her healing touch is delicately distributed, and of that I have no doubt. Now when I look back I see how Lourdes seemed to have followed me my whole life. My original home parish in the county of Carlow, Ireland has a huge replica of the Lourdes Grotto; where Our Lady appeared to St. Bernadette Subirous in 1858, as too did the rehab I had attended.

> At the heart of Lourdes stands an encounter of love between a child and a Mother, a child Bernadette Soubirous and Mary, Mother of God and our Mother. That meeting happened a long time ago in 1858. It was a sacred and special moment that would forever change the face of a small French village, reach way beyond the Pyrenees, reawaken the spiritual yearnings of people from every corner of the earth and make Lourdes what it is today, a worldwide center of pilgrimage.[1]

These were not mere coincidences but an assurance of Our Lady's presence throughout my entire life. She and Lourdes discreetly awaited me. I am very touched to be living here. Geographically, the majesty of the Pyrenees which surrounds Lourdes gives God his voice in nature. He screams from the mountain tops. I only had to open my bedroom window to see him every morning, God seemed to be everywhere I looked. It is no surprise I felt immediately at home there. Lourdes helped to heal me—inside and out, and for that I am eternally grateful. I had the time, opportunity and space to spiritually grow and evolve here. I even was gifted the company of a beautiful little dog, who I aptly named "Molly" (Irish for Mary), in honor of the Madonna. The dog has proved to be my constant companion and she is a therapy in herself. She is the joy of my life. Words could never explain the relationship I have with the little dog I was given in Lourdes. But I also was generously gifted the beauty of true friendship there, and this helped cement my attachment to the place. True friends are hard to come by and I was given a gem. God gave me all I needed to make a life here. I shudder to think of me not taking the risk by coming here, and I question where I would be now if I had not. Would I have returned to my old ways?

---

1. John Lochran, *The Miracle of Lourdes: A Message of Healing and Hope*, (Ohio: St. Anthony Messenger, 2008), 2.

It frightens me to think how fear of the unknown could have hindered me from following my gut, and how dependency on the familiar would have kept me in another jail of sorts. Had I ignored what God had in store for me, had I not taken that opportunity to come here, my Spirit would never have been free to soar high. Another world opened up for me, another way of life presented itself to me, and I do not mean strictly the French lifestyle. I mean another way of "being" was realized for me, and that "being" is grounded in Spirit. My awareness expanded and I am now anchored in God and committed to spirituality, as a source of wholeness which cannot be found anywhere else. My definition of "spirituality" grew, no longer confined to a relationship with God, but it embodies all of me: body, mind, and soul. I realize now that everything in life is spiritual. Yes, my spiritual growth is an ongoing process, a life-long work in progress if you will, but it defines me and grounds me; it gives meaning to my life. Nothing else can replace it. I have learned a lot on my journey. I have befriended many saints, lit many candles and said many prayers, ran many laps, and read many books, and I do not plan on changing any of that any time soon. What I have created for myself is in fact a lifestyle lived in God, and it has worked wonders for me. This is why I felt the need to tell my tale. I have taken myself from wreck to wonderful wholeness via this route, and I noticed along the way that if I had neglected any one part of my journey, that I would have been depriving myself of something. Everything that I have learned and have found of help in my evolvement fitted into its own place; everything had a reasoning behind it, one step led to another and each step complimented and built on what had gone before. Growth involves pain, but you gain the courage to shed your old ways and build something new for yourself, something much better. It is very true that to those whom have been given much, more will be given. It is those who make the effort to seek out Truth, transformation, or enlightenment that receive, because they actually look for it. It is like a student of medicine. Through study they will learn more and receive more knowledge. The same is true for those who seek God and wholeness. It won't come to you unless you make a conscious effort and persist in that. Nobody takes the gold medal without consistency in their training.

Leaving the false boundaries of our ego behind to search for enlightenment allows for all kinds of limitless possibilities to emerge. Transcendence can be called the final frontier. Yet it is not final; it is only the beginning of another stage in your life, a more fulfilling stage. Hell would be to not have faith, to do little and to believe our lives are limited. Do not underestimate your capacity; do not live a wasted life, when we are unlimited because we have God's creativity within us. This creativity allows for more control in your life. You call the shots rather than being played by life; then, you essentially become a co-creator, and you gain direction in your own life. No longer are you floating aimlessly, adrift like a bobbing log being carried along by life's watery currents. You start to power your own sail and take responsibility for your life. Being whole allows for all that and more. But you must do it. You must start. Empower yourself with your own personal power that comes from being in connection to God. Trust your intuition and your own inner GPS. Baby steps are sufficient until you come to stand confidently on your own two feet. God will guide you once you start, it is as simple as that; you have nothing to lose and a better life to gain. The fruit is there and ripe for the picking. Have faith in God, as "with God all things are possible" (Matt 19:26).

Chapter 2

False Starts

When a gift horse stares you straight in the face, it is better to smile back at him rather than hit him between the eyes. I stupidly had hit that gift horse many times and had told him to "feck off, I don't need you" or "I am grand, thanks." Heaven knows I had done that many times in the past, but this time it was different. Like many before me and many more to come, I had to hit rock bottom before I recognized the glint that was in that horse's eye. Realizing once and for all that the poor horse was not an old annoying nag, but a gem of a gift, took time. But that realization did come. It was only then that I mounted that horse and rode off into the sunset, so to speak. It was an old-fashioned rescue of course, just like how I imagined as a child, but my hero was not a knight in shining armour—yes, the metaphorical horse was there, and it goes without saying that the setting was perfect: my fairy tale dress flowed down over the horse's saddle like a waterfall in spring, birds sung all around as the golden sun set—but my hero was nowhere to be seen. He was not even visible, and some suggest he does not even exist. I beg to differ, as my hero was God. It took time and a lot of research for me to come to understand that not only did I have this "superhero" known as God to rescue me, but I had in fact rescued myself, as God is also within me. God is in everything and is everywhere. I had attributed my rescue or my SOS to a God who I believed was somewhere out there, not realizing that I myself held the key to my own destiny. My journey from wreck to wonderful wholeness has been an experience, one of growth and profound astonishment at how God's universe really works, and happily I am still learning and still loving it. I learned over time that awareness of God or the sacred in life creates a presence that leads not only to self-knowledge, spiritual expansion, and growth, but it also holds the key to finding true, genuine happiness that comes from within and not from the outside. Spiritually sleepwalking through our lives only enables life's disillusions to remain, and for us to remain stuck in our own kind of fish bowl, circling in muddy waters. But how does one awaken from such a deep slumber? How to stop circling in those muddy waters and start swimming upstream? What is spiritual awareness anyhow, and why should people care about it? What are we looking for and how do we recognize it? It all sounds very deep and mysterious.

For me now God/Spirit is my newest addiction. It is like cocaine—the more I get, the more I want and the more I need to feel my veins pulsating with this presence. It is drug-like, but a life-giving drug as opposed to life-strangling, life-stagnating, life-stealing drug. I was lucky I was receptive to the spiritual in life, but this I always knew. Even as a child I felt a deep connection to heaven, to God, and to the natural world. Being born into a rural setting left an organic and very natural connection to the earth, with its seasons bringing forth birth and death, nature's highs and lows, the seasonal pendulum swinging, bringing rhythm to life and life to rhythm. It was a blessing to be a witness of this, and is a privilege to be a participant. It is a marvelous miracle to be part of this natural phenomenon that we can so often take for granted, to be placed within this universe, to breathe its life-giving energy force into our bodies each and every second of the day. Life is miraculous no matter what form it takes. To use economic or selfish reasoning to undermine life is not good for humanity or the universe in which we live. Coincidentally, we so often conveniently forget that we are codependent upon that same universe. "Forgetfulness" is a global epidemic, crossing cultures and continents. We forget the most basic principles, those of primary importance to us as a species, without which we will not survive. Self-destruction on a planetary basis is ironic, considering we classify ourselves as "intelligent" beings. The irony is sadly not funny, as we literally are destroying ourselves not only as individuals, but as a planet within our solar system. Single-handedly we can potentially wipe ourselves out. We really are still living from a primal and immature standpoint; when it comes to our responsibilities to the planet and as rational beings, this should not be the case. We are very unique, indeed. Yet life is a gift freely given, and therefore it should be respected for that alone, if nothing else. Sadly, too many people miss the point and resent life as cruel and miserable, creating more misery by their miserable attitude, brought on mostly by materialism.

Simple gratitude can be overlooked. Our global greed is also brought on by materialism; globalization and unfair distribution of the Earth's plentiful resources, creating economic and social imbalance and hardship. Materialism is indeed a modern evil that risks ruining western society's peoples. It is like a disease that is spreading globally, slowly but surely into every cell of society across the world. It is frightening to see how people are sucked into believing that "things" will make them "happier," "better," "healthier," "thinner," "more beautiful" people, when that is in fact a complete lie that has absorbed so many, especially the young. Yet we are already completely perfect in every possible way. God does not create imperfectly, and never did. The perfect example is of a simple, yet-complex snowflake's classic beauty: its perfection and individuality is, namely, "classic" for a reason. The reason be-ing that the Creator creates in a manner that is incomprehensible to us. We still do not understand even the tip of the iceberg of our very own brain's functioning. We think we know it all, we see only that which we want to see, and choose to ignore those things which we only *think* do not interfere directly with our daily lives. We do not care if a rain forest was cut down in order that we have exotic foods on our plate. We just want what is on the plate. Who questions how it got there? We can change the channel so as not to watch the hungry refugee looking back at us in our reclining seats in our sitting rooms, while we eat half and throw away the other half of our chemically-laden dinners before we go to the gym to burn off the fat from our supermarket's "sweet treat special offer," or to go the cinema to look at an even bigger TV. The news and images of wars and famines in other countries had a numbing effect on us. Images that have appalled us in the past gather no more attention than the ads or the weather. Sadly, we seem to have become almost immune to these images. Images of profound poverty and sadness now leave us almost complacent. As parents and children give more time, money and interest over to the video games that glamorize war and destruction, rather than to real events. Images of violence have sadly become first nature to our younger population, which is subsequently also the next generation. To a large degree, we have become a self-interested and self-serving consumerized population of people. I may be painting a very bleak picture, but it is true for the most part of Western society. We have as a people gone too far in one direction and have forgotten that life is a process inclusive of all creation, not a manufactured lifestyle. We have forgotten the magical and true essence of life.

This sacred process, which *is* life, is given to us from a loving Creator, who intended life to be a pleasure; to hold meaning and hold a sense of purpose for us. We do not to want to kill ourselves on a commercial, material, and false treadmill, which is void of any true life-giving creative energy. We want and need meaning in our lives. We want to be fulfilled. Sitting in a spa drinking green tea, eating healthy organic foods, exercising, or doing yoga do not make us the happiest of people on their own. Yes, we emerge rejuvenated and yes, all are very necessary to create a healthy and better life for us, but without the element of Spirit, of connecting with God, we are still left with a huge void to fill. This emptiness needs to be understood and filled. We are spiritual beings having a human experience, not humans hoping to have a bit of a spiritual life, and once you understand this you can start to grasp the whole meaning of life and really start to enjoy living it. Knowledge is power, as they say, and this "power" is within you. It does not come from anything outside of you. In fact, we are looking at life from the wrong perspective. We think we are looking at life from the inside out, but we are in fact looking at life from the outside in. It is the body that is within the mind, and not the mind that is within the body. We are inside out, so to speak, yet we do not realize it.

God is an intelligent, life-giving energy force and this life-giving creative energy is here for us all. We just have to be aware of it and work with it, not against it. We need to "turn on" the switch in our heads that has been left off for too long. This may have been no fault of our own, but sadly mankind has passed on and inherited an egocentric mentality that has brought us to the brink of despair. This "me, myself, and I" mentality has created all the fear and pain-based emotions within us and this of course has filtered and trickled down through the ages. Fear of lack, fear of foe, fear of whatever fantasy enters our minds; all are created by ourselves and need to be deconstructed and rebuilt to demonstrate how we can create and live a different kind of life for ourselves and others.

I was not always spiritually aware. I "lost" myself for twenty-three years. I was lucky to be rudely awakened from my so-called sleep walk of a life and coincidentally found myself. What I found was not the same old self, but a new and improved version of the older model, so to speak. This self, my true self, was better built than the previous production. In fact, I had been upgraded for a newer model. This one has six gears instead of five and was turbocharged. This model was more roadworthy and better equipped to handle the roadways of life. This model runs on special fuel that's free, efficient, and eco-friendly; fuel that is manufactured by a company not visible to the naked eye, yet has a bountiful, infinite, and abundant supply. My fuel had been hidden inside me all along, where it was lovingly supplied by the "gas company" of God. I found that I could now perform better all around. I was my own vehicle, restored and renovated; it was that simple. Ditching old habits came easily as I started to change my thinking and entrusted everything to God. I could clearly see that since I kept his company I was doing well. I was running on all five cylinders. I was fueled for life, and life was for living. I began to truly live my life for the first time ever. I had finally taken off, but this time it was different. This time I was going in the right direction and I had a great interior navigation system to guide me. There was and still is no turning back. If I could bottle it, I would be a millionaire, yet I am already rich beyond my wildest dreams. This is ironic, of course, as I have the least amount of money I have ever had in my life, yet it feels great. "Things" no longer hold my interest. What interests me now is the spiritual life. This is the one and only true life; this provides real personal power. Some may think that's nuts, but I do not care. I have moved from being a drunk with no life quality at all, to person with a newly-found blissful life living in conjunction with Spirit. Faced with desolation, isolation, and emotional dysfunction, I metaphysically was dead on all levels. Physically a toxic time bomb ticked inside me, within the drunken, disillusioned, death-enabling calamity of a life I myself had created. Calamity is probably the best way to describe how life was for me when I drank and was cut off from God. I now see how being separate from God is the biggest lie that anyone of us can live. We cannot be separate from God; this is a fact that I learned the hard way. Yet to fully realize this I had to do the classic lifestyle three-hundred and sixty degrees turn-around, otherwise I would not have appreciated it for what it was. One has to know winter to appreciate the summer; one has to experience the pain to appreciate pleasure; and one has to sink before one can learn to swim. I was very good at sinking. I sank down into depths I never knew even existed.

I was in a dungeon for twenty-three years until I gave in and gave my life to God. Faith and perfect timing played their part too to get me to that point where I saw real meaning in my life. It was no coincidence that I was where I was at any given time; God's hand was there turning the winder on my time piece, and my wakeup alarm happened at the perfect time. He knew when and how to act. I was not Paul of Tarsus, nor Constantine the Great, but my awakening came nonetheless. This was such a gift to reinstate myself, a God-given gift to help me become the whole person I was born to be. The scales were lifted from my eyes and I could see correctly for the first time. The waters in my murky fish bowl began to clear. The chance emerged to become whole again, free from the shackles I had chained myself in. This was my opportunity to shake them off and face a new horizon, a new beginning, and a second chance at life. The new sky brought with it unimaginable beauty, Truth, and goodness. Abundant life was there for the taking—not only for me, but for all who are willing to be open to it. I saw life through a different lens, in a new and brighter light, and I liked what I saw. This did not happen overnight, but over time.

But with that time, all of life emerged into an even more profound magnificence for me. The experience of life itself, be that good or not so good, swelled into an ocean of life-learned lessons. Life has thought me how to live and God has been my professor. I have to add that he has been the most surprising of teachers, imparting me with skills I never knew existed nor knew I possessed. He gave me one hell of a roller coaster ride. The best part was that it was for free. No ticket was needed. This left me with a serious sense of how we can easily overlook or even underestimate our own unique life experiences to our very detriment if left unexamined or taken for granted. If we can just push ourselves past our comfort zones, dig deep, and mine from within, we can learn more from all our great Professor has to teach us. Life is great when perceived from higher perches and that is no exaggeration. But how can we climb to such spiritual heights? How can we get a sneak peek of a vision which we struggle to even comprehend? The secret is simple: curl up closer to our Creator, allowing him to enter into a closer relationship with us. By doing so we invite and open the floodgates of God's light to illuminate our thinking and our lives. It allows for expansion, for our world to open up within us. It is a simple path, really; all it requires is that one is open to God. Once you are receptive to God in your life, the relationship can nurture and grow, giving and taking as God's love pours out and as you give back in return. No relationship is one way—our vehicle is on a two-way street. God will fuel you and direct you via your interior GPS but you have to learn to drive it, to handle it, to maneuver it, and to be willing to take a few driving lessons. Like anything in life, a little bit of time and effort is required. Nothing happens by magic. You don't wake up one morning and have spiritual enlightenment by accident. Those who are spiritually aware, those who are fully awake to their true spiritual identity, are so by effort. They invest time into seeking out God and a deeper meaning to life. They look past surface illusions to find Truth. Life then begins to hold more depth, more meaning and certainly more pleasure. One sees more clearly the magnificence of this universe and all that is in it. This in turn brings people true joy and happiness, as security comes to those who no longer are held hostage by the fears of life. Fear goes out the window in the certainty that we are directly connected to a God who is not only capable of holding up planets such as Jupiter and Mars, but also holds us. Fear of death disappears as we realize that death is only a doorway to another existence and it is in this other existence where reality really lies and where we really belong.

Chapter 3

One Giant Step for Mankind

W e all basically want to be happy in life and to be loved; this is human nature. We differ in how we go about achieving our objectives, but our basic primary goals in life remain the same for the most part. I took the scenic route, as a lot of people do, but it is so easy to get lost and stray off the path that leads to fulfillment and wholeness. It can be an uphill struggle for most people. Nobody waltzes through life all the way; there are always bumps, stops, and starts. It is what makes life worth living, falling down and getting up again. We learn from experience. It has a magic all of its own. Mistakes that we make can be the magic to transform us into better people. Struggles and setbacks give us strength, and heartbreaks hasten our courage and compassion toward others and can offer companionships otherwise never experienced. It is true what they say—every cloud does have a silver lining, even if it is not visible immediately.

God knows what he is about. Nothing is random and we experience life lived and learned in a manner that no textbook can ever teach us. Life is indeed *the* Open University. Where I thought happiness was to be found took me off my path and into huge potholes that took me years to climb out of. But I did indeed climb out and God gave a lifeline—once I asked, of course. There was a phone-a-friend option here, but I had to take it for myself and no one else, and once I got my head around that, everything else fell into place. It was the first act of self-love that I had undertaken in over two decades. I self-gifted myself to myself, without even realizing what I was doing at the time. Something acted in me. Something gave me the will to want to live; it was my True Self, and even though it was well buried, I could still make out its faint voice. I did not know what life was going to be for me, nor did I know what to expect, but it did not disappoint me. I am not unique; anyone with eyes can see, anyone who has ears can listen, anyone who wants to participate, can. All you have to do is act. What was there for me is there for all and sundry to enjoy also. God's house is an open house, one with a door that's open; you do not even have to knock to enter, you just have to walk right in. But it's up to you to get your foot inside the door. Motivating oneself to take that step that might as well be "one giant leap for mankind" for a lot of people. But it is never that scary. It is a homecoming after all. I was like a child that had run away from home. I was never at ease and never knew why, until I realized that I was in fact "homesick." The sickness left when I walked back in the door and once again greeted my Creator. Being back home I was at instantly at ease in my own skin and fell backwards into his embrace, knowing full well that I was indeed safe, fully supported, and secure. Nothing could harm nor would harm me ever again. It was a complete and utter loss of my egocentric self and a reunion with my True Self. I reclaimed my divine identity, as I had lost it along the way in a sea of distortion. I had been lost in a delusion, but allowing God's energy to resurface and a return of self-love and self-trust to enter into my life saved me. This process took time, and I gave myself that time. I needed to heal, to become whole again, for what I am speaking about did not come like a bolt of lightning but rather like a flower blossoming.

First, I was in the right mindset—I was ready for a transformation. I needed it and I wanted it. I knew my life could be different and I had to change. I wanted to feel alive. The intent was there, and it progressed into actions. The seed had been planted in my head and in my heart. Later, I was watered and fed by the right environment and conditions; these enabled me to see and feel again, and to start taking responsibility for my own life once more. A three-month stint in an excellent residential rehabilitation clinic for alcohol addiction in Ireland, called *Cuan Mhuire,* kickstarted my healing process, allowing me to physically and mentally detox from my toxic life style. Spirituality played an important role in that rehab to allow for a whole recovery of body, mind, and soul. This was critical, as they had not ignored the role of Spirit and God on the road to recovery. If that vital link had been ignored or downplayed, I would not be talking to you today. Slowly, my eyes and heart reopened. I began to feel good about myself; what I saw and what I felt came from God, from simply being connected to myself again and to he who is in me. I did not have the capacity to see this immediately, of course, as I was occupied just getting sober, but I eventually realized what had taken place during my time of healing. I grasped that God really does give to those who ask, to those who seek. The more receptive I was, the more he gave.

God is not just good; he is very good. His love knows no bounds. I used to think phrases like that were really tacky, until I realized that they are actually very true. I did not during my initial days in rehab call on God specifically for help, as back then I did not truly know God. I only knew of him, but not in person. It was my own willingness to continue further with my transformation that instigated this "heavenly" collaboration between what one can call heaven (or the spiritual realm, or the divine consciousness, or the non-local intelligence, or the supernatural) and myself. It was a subconscious call to my Creator, my Source, my "True" self on an intimate and inner deep level. Somewhere within me a longing for change outgrew my old self and my old way of being; I had had enough of being lost and desolate. It was a do-or-die scenario, and I chose life. So by meeting God in the middle ground we finally got to become properly acquainted. I slowly but surely began to ask heaven for help. When I realized that what I was doing was actually really working, I started to sit up and really take notice, and not surprisingly I began to take the spiritual life a lot more seriously as well. What rehab had done for me, besides detoxing me from alcohol, was to challenge my old habitual perspectives and, it brought back God into my life. Whether I liked it or not religion was part of the agenda in rehab and it ironically has become the most important element of my entire focus. I am eternally indebted to that rehab.

I make it all sound so easy, and it can be once you stop being so hard on yourself. One does not have to be religious or spiritual to start having a relationship with oneself or God. One does not need to know the answers to life's mysteries, nor to understand the secrets of the universe, in order to trust that universe. Just take the time to stand still in silence. Giving yourself precious time alone with God in meditation will allow you to block out life's distractions and you will be able to hear your soul. If that feels organic and sits comfortably in one's heart, it is a firm indication that you are on the right track. We all have our own built in GPS, or "God's Protective System," that is in built in us by our divine nature. God is in us, we are part of him and he is part of us; therefore, his characteristics are there within us—it is just a matter of discovering them, as we have been experts at disguising our true identity and nature. We are, in fact, God's children, and are carrying the same Spirit or essence as the Creator of creation. When you are not going with God and not following with his GPS, you do get those nagging sub-conscious feelings that something is amiss, that you are unhappy, that something is not right, that all is not as it seems. You actually have a gut feeling that something is wrong, offline, not quite sitting as it should be within you. Your conscience is actively mulling over things and you are not at peace internally. There is a constant unease within you, within the situation and within your life. It amounts to inner turmoil and suffering, and can amount to emotional torture, manifesting itself in many ways and eventually into your physical self in the form of illness. These are all symptoms of separation from God, from self, and from the universe. Symptoms of being dismembered, of being disabled or unplugged from Source, so to speak. We have become disjointed, while in fact we are not separate but one. We are separately part of the whole, we are a segment of an orange, if you like. Many segments form the orange, and oranges come from a tree, which is rooted in the ground; that ground is on this earth, placed within this universe. Everything and everyone is interconnected. To disconnect from our source; from God, from nature, from each other, is to literally cut ourselves off. You are effectively cutting off your nose to spite your face, or cutting a finger from your hand. These sentiments are not some new age hippie talk, but a known fact since the time of the pharaohs. This is not some dressed up twenty-first-century new age stuff, but fact.

Quantum science, (dealing with atoms and photons in quantum states as opposed to the classical; Albert Einstein contributed to quantum theory in a 1905 paper[1]), has verified for us that energy connects all in the universe and that we are all essentially made of the same stuff; we are but masses of energy. Therefore, by loving each other, we are loving ourselves, because as we send out good energy to others in the form of loving positive thoughts, we are accorded the same in return. Thoughts are waves of energy; this energy creates positivity or negativity. It is a simple equation of physics; thoughts are things that manifest into reality. It is why Jesus very importantly commanded us to love one another, and he had very good reasoning, because not only is it the correct way to behave, but also it makes life much easier on ourselves, others, and society at large. It creates individual, group, and global consciousness of a high and good quality. It is the recipe for global peace and love. Jesus did not have a highly educated audience back in Roman-occupied Israel, nor had quantum science been explored yet, so he spoke as simply and as plainly as he could. Jesus's philosophy on love is actually scientifically proven as we begin to advance in the field of energy research and quantum physics. Religion perhaps has placed Jesus Christ on a very high divine pedestal. But perhaps this pedestal rose far above people's heads to allow the brilliance of what he spoke over two thousand years ago to properly shine through. Scientific advancement ironically cannot beat the mastery of delivery of the teachings of Jesus, but it confirms what he

---

1. "Albert Einstein: Quantum Theory," *SparkNotes*, sparknotes.com/biography/Einstein/section9.rhtml.

said and how it is energetically possible. Jesus operated at a higher energy level than us; our energy is sadly slowed down by the many toxic thoughts we possess.

When the Creator creates he does so perfectly. This universe is not some random act, but a perfectly orchestrated symphony; it is ordered and managed, right down to the very last detail. The loving order of the universe can be understood in manners of mathematics, science, and creativity. For me, God is the master scientist of them all, a loving, creative energy. The concept of an old man on a throne does no longer wash with me, and I imagine for most adults today this image of God is also outdated. Our understanding of God had to start somewhere, but the trick is not to continue to hold this image of an old man on a throne. Rather, let our understanding evolve, grow, and mature. As our life deepens and develops into differing layers of experience, this too should be echoed in our relationship with God. The God you heard about or perhaps feared as a child should not be the same God you hold in adulthood. Your relationship with God should shift and mature, as does any long-term relationship. Nothing remains stagnant, and neither should our image or relationship with the divine or our spirituality. If it has not, then it is time to rethink your image of God and your place in the world in relation to him.

Self-love does not come very easy for a lot of people. Many sessions have been spent with psychologists trying to disembowel a person's distorted self-image and sense of self. Destructive thinking, creating malignant manifestations in people's heads, has unfortunately left a lot of people with not just a confused sense of self, but also of others. If people just remembered or revisited their notion of self which was given by God, many a sofa would be left empty, and many a psychiatrist would be unemployed or not needed at all. God simply made us perfect, whole, and complete. By not loving his perfect, whole and complete creation, we are rejecting not only ourselves, but also his love, as God is within us. God experiences himself in and through us. This is why we feel so good when we are connected to him; we have, in fact, found ourselves, our true identity. Self-love reunites us with not only ourselves, but with others and God. When I speak of our connection with God or reuniting ourselves with him, I am not talking about some superficial level of communication, or some gesture of reappearing at church at Christmas, or the weekly attendance at church to fuel us for the week. No, I am talking about a genuine mature attempt to connect with God on an authentic and conscious level. This is where church has failed. People do not feel fulfilled, and the idea of church and organized religion does not sit comfortably with everyone. Self-exploration and self-education are a must, and this is where books, courses, and the internet can be a great asset. Exploration is a huge help in finding enlightenment; by reading you can relate to a particular author's style and delivery very well, and learn a lot. Teachers come in all shapes and forms, be open to all that is available to you; after all, there is a lot out there. Be open to growing, to evolving, to expanding your vision and understanding.

In fact, we never stop learning, be that from life itself or from our own efforts. The day we cease to learn is the day we die, for to learn is to live. Thankfully, society has at least become more compassionate, open, and honest. Changes in recent years have enabled society to move forward at a very fast rate, both for good and for ill. But essentially what we have today is a better, more aware, mature spiritual seeker. Today's spiritual seekers are not mere conformists to rites and ritual, to hierarchical handouts or fears, but operate from an authentic level of questioning and enquiry. Today's spiritual seekers want and need to be true to themselves and their motives for religious practice. If they practice at all, that is; the understanding of religious practice is very narrow at times. People's notion of religion and spirituality has become confused and muddled. Spiritual identity has been lost and religious abandonment has increased. Formal religious practice is not spirituality and the two need to be identified and understood for what they are, as misunderstanding creates only distance and more misunderstanding, resulting in added distances. People need to be comfortable with spirituality and to understand that it is not a thing to be frightened of or to shy from. Spirituality is our own connection to God, to Spirit within us; that is our core being, our essence. The only fears we have are those that we create ourselves in our own minds—these then keep us running on that dreaded treadmill that rotates constantly in our egocentric minds.

To not connect with Spirit, to not acknowledge our universe as divinely structured, or to deny our divine origin as given by God is to deny our very own foundation. It is the same as denying your very own parentage, your heritage. But we as a people are God's creation; it is only by the act of his creating that we too can create. This is our essence, and it is what we create that affects our quality of life; our very happiness depends on it. Unfortunately, we let our egocentric fears take charge over our lives, and many look to the outside to find that happiness, when we already have it inside of ourselves: it is God in us. We possess the very thing we are looking for all along. It is right under our noses, but we refuse to see it. We end up giving ourselves *nose jobs*, instead of recognizing ourselves as already perfect, whole, and complete. God is the way to true happiness, and when you're happy on the inside it shows on the outside. You then realize you do not actually need that expensive nose job after all.

God wants us to be happy. He even saw we were not so quick at this game of life and sent us lots of teachers over the centuries to help us. We have been told numerous times what to do to make life easier on ourselves. But unfortunately we did not listen. We hear all right, but we do not fully digest, nor do we want to put into practice what we have heard. We find these religious stories and fables very favorable, but we can be more concerned about who sees us at church, or who we will meet up with after church, than what went on *in* the church itself. We dress our children up like Barbie and Ken to receive sacraments. We live in a culture where the after party is more important than the actual ceremony. Everybody openly admits this, it is no secret that the communion money means more to the kids, as they recognize the money for its worth, but they have little recognition of the spiritual. How could they, really? After all, they are only kids, but sadly the same applies to most parents and adults—they have had no real experience of the divine in their lives. Again, like the kids, it is not completely their fault.

Historically the way religion has been taught in the west has not been a grand model of success. Jesus Christ (just one of the great teachers God sent us) himself appeared to be anti-hierarchical, anti-patriarchal and anti-hypocritical in his treatment of the existing religious organization of his time, yet we molded Christianity upon Jesus's teachings and came out with the very system that he had opposed. It is no surprise that Christianity as an organized religion has remained, but also has historically struggled. Yet, Christianity has stood the test of time. It has never gone away, and this may be due in part to economic gains that the Christian church brought, but also to the fact that a lot of genuine people over the centuries thought that Jesus had been on to something— that he had in fact spoken some sense. These people became good Christian role models. They saw how Jesus in his methodology showed us how to attain fulfillment in life. This "fulfillment" can be summed up in one word: "love." Love is the key. Lack of love is the root of all problems within life and society. If we simply put more love into everything and everyone, we would be so much better off. We have an endless supply of love within us, yet we store it up, never allowing ourselves to reach our full potential as human beings. We are afraid to share our true feelings, and therefore to be left exposed and vulnerable. We might lose something instead of gaining, is our conditioned mentality. We are hoarders. We hoard stuff, and we also hoard our true feelings and emotions. Fear of showing others our true thinking or our intent keeps us as the unhealthy egocentric people we have become. We fear not having enough even though we create mountains of unwanted food on a daily basis; being afraid of not accumulating enough or acquiring enough is how we have historically been conditioned to live. Competitive behavior is evident in all sections of society, from our schools to our work ethics, from our games to our social clubs, from breast seizes to the number of shoes we possess, from our cooking abilities to our cars. All of life has become an acquisition of some sort. It keeps the treadmill turning, and we have allowed ourselves to become ferrets chasing nothing but our tails. It is hard to see where the love is in a society obsessed with acquisition. So much energy is wasted on making a good living in order to comfortably acquire more stuff to make us happy. But ironically most people are not happy, or they pine after the things that they think will make them happy, saying things like "If only I had a bigger car," or "if only I had more money to go on more holidays," or "if only I was thinner and more beautiful," or the classic "if only they loved me and was with me my life would be complete . . . " Ladies and gentlemen, we are already wonderfully whole and complete. We do not need or require exterior factors for us to feel happy. It is a well-known fact that true happiness lies within. If I seem to be repeating myself it is because I indeed am. I say these obvious statements again and again, as so few of us fully understand the consequences of what is being said. We have the power and ability to live our lives in perfect bliss; of that have no doubt. Trust that this perfect universe in which we live is ready and willing to respond to you right now. This divine universe is a pulsating presence and you are part of that presence. Acknowledge that and all will be well for you. Reconnect with Spirit that is within you. Open your eyes and look out your window. See the beauty that is all around you. See beauty in your children's eyes, in the eyes of your pets, in the eyes of strangers, in your potted plant, in the night sky, in the dirty nappy, in the dirty washing, in the cooking of wonderful God gifted food, in the summer sun, in the winter snows, in comforting the crying child. See the miracle that is in all of life itself and remember where that life came from. It came from our divine creator, God. God gives all freely to you on silver platter; all you have to do is choose life, and that's it. By choosing life you, in fact, choose God, as the two are one and the same. You do not need to be in a spiritual place, as Spirit is all around you. It is everywhere and in everything. It is life itself. Fall in love with life itself and life will love you back.

Your inner joy and happiness radiates within God's universe and that universe responds to you. Jesus showed us how to love each other, how to love this life, and he did that via love. He gave freely, he needed nothing, and he simply loved and got love in return. He acknowledged and loved God, and loved people. He was the ultimate party person who excluded no one. He demonstrated how to do it, he turned the social norm of his time upside down, and he did it in style. He never doubted himself, but did all gracefully. He restored people; giving them back their emotional dignity, their health, their well-being, and most importantly, their faith in God. He never gave them a few bob for their conformation. He never rewarded people in a material fashion. One does not see Jesus handing out bills for the five loaves and five fish, plus tax. No, anything that God gives is freely given—his teachers included. A God who cares so much for our well-being will never abandon us, but we must acknowledge him and ask for help. God gave us free will; therefore he cannot and will not interfere without our consent; free will is a universal law. Jesus said the same; *ask*. It is that simple. Ask, trust that God will help you, detach from the outcome, and it is done. Leave it to God and do not worry.

But I at times am reluctant to even mention the name of Jesus Christ, as he has been placed on such a divine pedestal, that his image is one of an unobtainable deity. He can be seen as the unreachable flawless face of the Son of God. He is upheld as the "only" son of God, while in fact we are all sons and daughters of God. Stiff statues of Jesus as a white bearded male evoke a nonresponse from many, I imagine. Well, they do nothing for me anyhow. Statues have a lot to answer for; they can repel or attract us depending on the manner in which they were made. The statue of the Christ taken from a seventeenth century European church model is not going to evoke a passionate response from every twenty-first-century church goer. Young children or adolescents are not going to warm to such images that do not fit into their modern mindset or imagination. The warm Jesus they learn of in school is not the same person who is coldly depicted in the church. The two just do not match. It is no wonder youngsters and people are confused. They feel isolated from Jesus, as clashing imagery of him exist in churches, art, and books. Beautiful as they are, modern associations with Jesus do not fit a lot of these old images still in use. Even film depictions of Jesus have been somewhat dubious at the best of times. Somehow he appears either as a creepy, mysterious hippie type or an overly pious, cold and distant figure, yet the man I read and hear about seems to be a different kind altogether. It took me a while to find him. I had to search hard. What I found, I also found I could relate to. Gone for me was the stiff statue, gone was the unobtainable deity of porcelain perfection. I found a real man who oozed tenderness without being soft. I found a man who for once spoke real Truth, and I found a real person who was obviously highly evolved, yet not cocky. He was "cool" in a way. This guy I could relate to.

Jesus held a different level of consciousness than those around him, an elevated consciousness, one that we are to strive toward. He showed us how life should be and can be for us. It is very obtainable if only we follow his way. What exactly was his way? As already mentioned, it simply boils down to love. Every spiritually aware person in history knew and knows that fact. Every world religion operates on the same premise of love in one manner or another. It is central to life, and without love there is no point to life. The universal laws of attraction work from love and positivity. By being centered in love, all of life works better. Jesus really was on to something when he spoke of loving one's neighbor. Jesus displayed no egocentric behavior and acted as his true self; we too are called upon today to do the same. It is not as mysterious as people think—to follow Jesus or to be fully Christian is to let go of your ego and work from your higher True Self. Psychology will tell you that, and hours of therapy will amount to the same thing. Saints over the centuries have done it—they stripped themselves of their egocentric behaviors and let go and let God. There they found true peace and happiness. Any twelve step program will tell you the same. Live simply and love lots is the key here.

Gratitude is another link in the chain of spiritual growth; it is part of a balanced equation, part of the give and take of life; God gives freely and we give thanks in return. It is like a domino; one has an effect on the other. It is a universal spiritual law. You acknowledge God, you praise him, you thank him and you ask for help if you need it. It is the complete circle of life that is ongoing and connected. A chain of links that are interconnected, as we too are all interconnected. The universe is one entity. When Jesus spoke of loving your neighbor, he did so because by loving your neighbor, you are consequently loving yourself in return. What you give out you get back. This is the universal and natural law at play again. These are laws not seen or written, but perennial universal laws. The universe operates under such laws, as it is ordered that way by God. Life is not simply haphazard. When God created it, he created perfection. Balance is beautifully portrayed within God's universe; it is demonstrated through polarization of opposites. For every day there is a night; for every spring there is an autumn; for every birth there is a death; and for every door that closes, there is another that opens. Life is constantly changing and evolving; as life is movement. But, it is only when we open our eyes and see the divine at work within our own lives and the universe, that that our existence finds real meaning. You can be alive and be "dead" to life at the same time by sleepwalking through life and not recognizing life for what it really is or for what we really are. This is detrimental to us as spiritual beings and for our spiritual development.

We are up to the neck in our own muddy waters, which are mostly created by our unwillingness to take what has been told to us seriously. Now, what has been said to us by organized religion,may have historically been done in a manner that has allowed the church to cut off its nose to spite its face. Yet, somehow a lot of people have managed to see past that and have not thrown out the baby with the bath water. Humans make mistakes; humanity has had a very long period of egocentric, male-dominated societies for centuries. It is only in the last fifty years that society has really started to change, and with that religion has changed too. We as humans are only starting to seriously evolve now, as society moves forward and traditional systems are questioned and brought forward for what they really were. Essentially, change is occurring rapidly, perhaps too much for some to fully comprehend that our past societies were set in an historical and social context. That is not to say that they were right or wrong, but it was merely where we were as a people at that given time in history, and our level of consciousness then. Mercifully, society did evolve, and growth took place. When I say "growth," I refer to an evolvement in consciousness, a shift that occurred. This shift happened faster in some places than others, and some places have not even begun yet. Different cultures and peoples change at various rates. But eventually, the final change will come to everyone, as group consciousness wins out. This can essentially be for the good or bad, but the good always outweights the negative; it is a natural law. By our very nature we lean toward the good and not the bad or the negative. It does not even have to be scientifically proven—people by nature desire good, desire love, and desire compassion. This is why feelings of intense interior unease, of being lost and unloved, create emotionally retarded people. It is because they have allowed the negativity to engulf them and they cannot see the good in the situation or the love in life anymore. It happens to us all at varying times, be it when we are very hurt, when we have suffered the loss of loved ones or just when life's twists and turns are too much to bear. It is how we deal with these periods that leads us on the road to either a bitterly-induced hell or an opportunity to grow and learn from the life lesson. It also depends where we are in this life—an adult of fifty years is (or should be) better emotionally equipped to deal with the loss of a loved one than a fifteen-year-old would be. Yet, the fifty-year-old can hit the bottle and the fifte-year-old can hit the boxing ring in the gym. Which do you think will come out better? Certainly it is the youngster who, by physically expressing their emotions, is in a better position than the one who literally "bottled up" his emotions. I know all about this, as I was a professional at it once. Nothing seemed like such a good idea as going for a pint and forgetting about life for a while. Blocking it out and getting plastered was always the best solution to any of life's problems that I encountered. Sure, it was great craic. But to say the least, I was not good at psychological self-analysis! Silence, hidden emotions, inadequacy, shame, bitterness, loss, anger, regret, and any other negative emotion that I had not dealt with halted me in my path. There I stood still for years, holding up bar stools and drowning out my pain; but unfortunately, this also drowned out and numbed my soul, my true essence, to near extinction.

Being separate from God and not falling into him, just the drowning of emotional pain, brought with it the full length color version of the cookbook of "recipes for disaster" for me. I was, in fact, *the* "master chef." I had mastered the art of being miserable. I was wretched, my family were miserably fed up of me, and my old dog was miserable too, I am sure. Why would he not be? I constantly breathed alcohol fumes down his neck, choked him with drunken hugs and blew cigarette smoke eternally into his big brown eyes. I am very surprised that the dog did not willingly run off; even a dog pound would have smelled better for him. How could anyone or anything that I encountered feel anything less than miserable? My wretched existence made everyone around me miserable too, unfortunately. My misguided presence affected everyone, but mostly myself, of course. What I had cooked up was nothing less than a time bomb, and I was ready to explode. The negativity that surrounded me was immense. I could not see the forest for the trees, yet I knew in my heart and soul that this was not who I was born to be. I knew that something was majorly wrong within me. As bad as my situation was, I could at least discern that. But I was only capable of this toward the very end, as things worsened immensely for me. My story is a divine comedy, and I have good reason to tell it. I want for people to realize the potential and benefits of being in union with God. I wish for people to experience all the good that life has to offer, and the interior peace that it brings. It is not total perfection, but a new way of living life to the fullest. Like anything in life worth doing, the more you put in, the more you get back. This has the benefit of affecting the people in your immediate environment positively and, of course, your beloved pets will not be wanting to run off. A life lived in partnership with God, built on foundations of love, is a winning recipe for a healthy life. God is here, God is your source, God is real, God is very much of use, and God is practical. This is not some senseless exercise in feeling "good," or feelings of some sort of hippie "high." A new partnership with God is going to help you in practical ways, as well as helping you to feel better within yourself, your life, and your place on this lovely planet of ours.

Being true to oneself is hugely important to our lives. God created us as individuals and as part of the whole. What keeps me ticking will most certainly not appeal to many, yet I have to honor my inner being, my uniqueness, and my journey in this life, as no one else can do that for me. The same goes for everyone. If we do not live a life that is in accordance with who we really are, we are only denying ourselves our inner Truth. This suffocates a person's personal growth and the soul's evolvement, allowing resentment to build; whether we are consciously aware of it or not, it creeps in. By following our God-given intuition, which can only be found through silence, meditation, contemplation, and prayer, we can come also to find our True-Selves. We enter a place where we can be who we were really born to be, a safe place where our divine origins are more obvious to us, as the everyday material world runs the risk of dissolving all knowledge of who we are due to being too caught up in it. Who we really are is pure Spirit; our interiority, or our souls, if you like, are nothing but pure Spirit. This Spirit yearns for freedom to create the life that we were born to live, a life that is not disconnected but continually connected and centered in Spirit, a life that falls back on heaven for help. When I say help, I mean the everyday mundane things and not just the huge decisions, or when things go wrong. It is extremely important for us as spiritual beings to continually seek heaven's guidanceand to thank heaven each day for all that we have and for its continued support. If you work in a job that you do not enjoy, instead of constantly complaining and moaning about it, appreciate it for what it is; that is, a stepping stone that pays the bills, a link in the chain of your life, an encounter with people who otherwise you would not have met. Try to see the good in your job and acknowledge it. Give thanks to the universe and heaven for all that it provides and at the same time ask heaven to help you to find a job that will be more fulfilling for you. Ask heaven for help to have the courage to change your job, change country, change the nappy, change boyfriends, or to simply have enough energy to drive the kids—whatever is needed for you in your life. Ask heaven for help to potty train the toddler who is having a difficult time changing habits. Connection with heaven is always there and it is open twenty-four seven. It is freely given once you ask and you don't even have to leave the house.

Being in connection to heaven will elevate your life, your way of thinking, and make you ultimately a more compassionate person. St. Teresa of Avila, in her poem titled "God Alone is Enough", wrote in her wisdom; "Whoever has God / lacks nothing: / God alone is enough."[2] This extra cushion that heaven can provide allows the path that you take, no matter where it will lead you, to be a smoother one. For, you are never alone. God is always there for you. God is your source. It is a very simple idea to grasp, but it remains true. Neither you nor I may know the complete workings of this magnificent universe, but we do not have to. Life is mystery. If we understood it all, it would be boring, cold, and clinical. Try doing an experiment and accessing heaven on a daily basis in some fashion; the method is not important, but it is the *intent* that's key here. Go to God, but go genuinely. Go wholeheartedly into his mystery. Give yourself to him, thank him, ask for guidance. It is not complicated. It will naturally come in time, as by our very nature we are all spiritual beings. There will come a day when by not connecting to your source you will feel a void, you will feel incomplete, you will feel insecure about life. We live in a society who has forgotten who they are, who has lost contact with their true spiritual identity and are in a vacuum of spiritual crisis. Modernity has largely lost or abandoned practicing their religions, but they have not been replaced in any manner other than materialism and autonomy. Community has suffered as a result. But religious "practice," if it had been done merely habitually or for the wrong reasons (other than falling in line) was probably of little or no use anyhow. Mere "practice" of religion does not give us the intimate relationship we need with God, or with ourselves.

Christianity has historically been so busy fighting inside itself over dogma and doctrine that it has neglected its inner journey and focused almost completely upon exterior behaviors and beliefs such as rites and rituals, political dealings, devotions, doctrinal writings, wars, and division. Thomas Merton (1915–1968), the

2. Teresa of Avila, "God Alone is Enough," 7–9.

twentieth century American Trappist monk, was among the first to publicly recognize the value of Christianity's lost traditions of contemplation and meditation:

> One of the first essentials of the interior solitude of which I speak is that it is the actualization of a faith in which a man takes responsibility for his own inner life. He faces its full mystery, in the presence of the invisible God. And he takes upon himself the lonely, barely comprehensible, incommunicable task of working his way through the darkness of his own mystery until he discovers that his mystery and the mystery of God merge into one reality, which is the only reality.[3]

Unfortunately, mysticism and mystics were viewed historically with suspicion, and personal contact with God was overshadowed by the egocentrically-based outer material world. It was easier to convey doctrine in black and white as opposed to the mysterious and supernatural. But in the present, we realize how Western traditions have missed out on the benefits of meditation and are delving deeper into our innermost depths. This is why people turned to Eastern traditions, such as Buddhism, to bridge that gap. They found within these traditions an element that they did not even realize existed within Christianity. It was always there—it just was never overemphasised or explored and, as I said, we were too busy within Christianity; we were occupied with the "real" world. Thankfully our follies are being reversed; as people are now witnessing a re-emergence of these traditions of contemplation, meditation, and inner silence practice. One cannot pass a book store without finding a well-being section promoting meditation, or a spirituality section without meeting the great contemplatives that Christianity has to offer, such as Julian of Norwich (1342–1416), St. Teresa of Avila (1515–82), St. John of the Cross (1542–91), St. Francis of Assisi (1181–1226) or Meister Eckhart (1260–1328), just to name a few. The re-emergence and the new found appreciation of the inner journey has happily moved religious experience

---

3. Thomas Merton, *The Power and Meaning of Love* (Great Britain: Ashford Color, 2010), 46.

from inside of church buildings to inside yourself and your inner temple, where God dwells. God cannot be confined to a place, or stuck within walls. We are starting to finally evolve as Christians. The Christian community is still very much needed, and authentic Christianity still needs to be practiced. But we also have our very own inner sanctuary: our soul. Our inner sanctuary is the most important of all churches. It is here where we find God within us and not without. St. Pio of Pietrelcina (1887–1968), noted how through the study of books one seeks God, and by meditation one finds him.[4] It is here where we can listen in stillness to our own inner GPS. Here we grow and evolve safely and in a place of peace when and where we choose. It is available to all, and the only thing you need is a conscious decision to practice it. "Practice" may seem like the wrong word here, but when I say "practice" I mean experiencing contact with Spirit on a regular basis. It is like checking in with your friends or calling your family. It is something that you do because you want to; otherwise there is a nagging sensation telling you that something is missing, that you are not happy, that you are incomplete and uncomfortable in your own skin. Again, these are classic symptoms of lack of divine contact. You see, when you work with Spirit, it works for you. It is give-and-take, with simple universal laws at work here in our material world. It is like the laws of gravity—you cannot see them, yet you know that they are there working for you. God's laws are the same. The clothes that you hang out on the line to dry stay up because you peg them there. Otherwise, by the laws of gravity they would fall down and be soiled. Simple. The giving or the receiving of divine help works by laws also. To receive you first have to give, and to give you first have to receive. Otherwise it falls in on itself like a house of cards. You simply have to build your house on a strong foundation and remain steady in your approach. Let Spirit be your gravity. By connecting with Spirit during your life, you build that strong foundation that is needed to house you, to ground you. Let Spirit be your strategy, and let everything follow from that. Build a life in unison

---

4. Mary Ellen Guiley, *The Quotable Saint* (New York: Facts on File, Inc., 2002), 172.

with God's Spirit, allowing for a new, better approach to life. Let this new approach incorporate God and his life-giving laws.

Sadly, the spiritual life, or spirituality and religious practice, has taken a back seat in our society. Emphasis is placed on the material, rather than the metaphysical or the supernatural. Meditation seems like a luxury rather than a necessity. Time spent cultivating our interiority seems to be under-valued and unappreciated for what it is. Spirituality is simply not seen as having any great practical use. It is better to spend two hours getting a color into our hair, absorbing toxins into our heads, rather than time spent soul searching or investigating our relationship with God and getting to know who we really are. The emphasis now is on the exterior rather than the interior and those now choosing the spiritual life are simply thought of as soft, naive, or wasting their time. Yet statistically those living a spirituality based career and life are among those who are the happiest in the world.[5] To focus completely on the exterior or the material world is creating an imbalance within us and adding to our unhappiness. We are both physical and spiritual beings. Not exercising or eating well are both going to affect our physical and psychological health, and the same applies to our spiritual health and well-being. We simply cannot afford to ignore any aspect of ourselves, as it is detriment to our well-being. What I am talking about is the original "trinity" of body, mind, and soul. The ancients knew it thousands of years ago, and now today we are trying to recover harmony and balance that we very much need in order to live healthy and happy lives. Shopping has replaced the Sunday church services, and inner reflection has been replaced by the TV. Of course it is easier to look at images of Paris fashion week and see who was wearing what and where, rather than to focus on our interiority. That said, there is nothing at all wrong with looking at fashion. I for one love it, but when our entire focus is solely set in the material world, we remain at a certain level of consciousness that is equivalent to a child's. We need to develop as God intended, and he wants for us to grow and not remain stagnant at a primitive

5. Charlene Adams, *Daily Mail*, dailymail.co.uk/news/article-2886974/study-religious-people-happier-life-satisfaction-others.html.

level. This is not because God is an angry God, who will punish us otherwise. No, it is because God is a loving God, who wants what is best for us. What is best for us is also best for God, as he discovers and experiences himself through us. I imagine that you would like your children to grow to their full potential and to not remain at the preschool level all their lives. Through the relationship you have with your kids, you also discover yourself. It is the same for God. He wants people to grow and expand in their thinking and knowledge. God wants us to live happier, easier lives because the way we live now, we are creating hardship for ourselves.

Chapter 4

Dive In

The highest and best experiences ironically are not of this material world, but of a different world, found in transcendence. Transcendence is a natural state of consciousness where the mind is completely silent yet alert. We "transcend" into God's frequency when we meditate, and it is there we find happiness and meet our souls in the stillness. Fashions may come and go, and while they of course add to our lives, they are not eternal. Eternal Truths though, are another matter. This world is passing away from us at each breath we take. Some of us will live long lives, and others will live shorter. Either way, one thing is for certain—we all will die some day, and as it was at our entry into this world, at death we too will be alone. This life is very short lived and passes by in an instant. How we choose to experience this life is completely up to us. What we can bring and what we can take from this life is up to us as individuals. You can be in what is considered a paradise and feel like you are in hell, or you can be in what is considered hell and feel like you are in paradise. It is all held in our minds and our approach to life. How we experience life is totally up to us, and it is how we interpret life that's important. You want the best for yourself—we all do. To be the best and to live life in the best possible manner we have to be whole and complete. It will give us a much better quality of life. This wholeness can only be found and fully realized within our connection to our source; namely, God. And the sooner this realization sinks into to our consciousness, the better life will become for all of us. This is why empty things do not fill us, why shallowness never satisfies, and these are only diversions from the Truth. Life has many diversions for us to lose our precious time over; delay tactics, if you want to call them that. Alcohol, drugs, materialism, busy lives, chasing your tail, and careerism are just a few samples of how life deludes us. Yet, some delay tactics do fill a very valid role for people and make them into who they are. My delay tactic was alcohol, and it allowed me to hit rock bottom and then to form a new and better appreciation of life. Not everyone has to go to such drastic measures in order to fully appreciate life, but diversions do abound. These diversions are very real, and "doing" as opposed to "being" has replaced living in a lot of cases. It is not what we "do" in life that counts, but "how we live" our lives as people, that is important. For example, you could be a successful heart surgeon, but abuse your station in life. Diversions and delay tactics will always be a part of life, it is to see past and through them that is the difficulty that people have. We have to remember that this world is only an illusion and a passing instant within a much larger picture.

In 2014, when on vacation for my Dad's eightieth birthday, I went scuba diving for the first time. I thought diving might be something interesting and decided to give it a go. But when I went under the water and entered into the deep mysterious world of the ocean, a simple realization hit me for the first time. I never would have realized from the beach I had just left behind that this magnificent world underneath the water had even existed. The stillness and beauty of it stunned me. I could have walked this earth for a hundred years and not have known that this sublime, silent submarine world had existed, had I not experienced it. That does not mean that it does not exist. Of course it does. I immediately felt validated. Just because something can be invisible to the naked eye at any given time, this does not mean it does not exist. It is very simple, really. This does not prove that God exists, of course, but for me, it was a huge help to have that experience, and to realize that things exist all around me, all the time, even though I do not see it. In my mind it is enough to vindicate things. But to only know that something exists and to experience it for yourself are completely two different things. Let us compare it to eating chocolate ice cream. If you have never actually tasted chocolate ice cream and discovered it for what it is, how do you know what it tastes like? How do you describe that to someone? You know it exists, but to experience it for yourself and its fabulous flavour will bring your taste buds to a new level, a new gourmet experience. God and spirituality are the same: until you try it for yourself, you do not know what you are missing. Until you allow yourself to eat from God's table or dive into his ocean, you cannot imagine the benefits or the spoils it will bring you. It is comparable to looking at the Grand Canyon on TV, as opposed to actually visiting it for yourself and experiencing that beauty and vastness of creation. That experience will fill you with awe and inspiration. "Just do it," as Nike says. It is a simple statement, yet it speaks volumes. There is no point in merely thinking about doing something, or merely being envious of another's disposition, be that physically, emotionally or spiritually. Action is what is needed. I see people who consistently admired traits in others, like their athletic figure, or their happy, sunny disposition. Although they are yearning for the same and envious of it, they do nothing to help themselves. They have the same life opportunities and knowledge about health, fitness, and well-being, yet they sadly do not do anything about it. It seemingly was easier to criticize from the sofa and begrudge people rather than to actually try to help themselves. To get fit you need to move your body or get involved in some kind of exercise. The same goes for people who find inner peace and illuminate with an inner joy. It does not happen by accident, but is acquired. It is acquired by remaining in constant and consistent contact with your inner divinity, your interiority, and your relationship with God and with yourself. In fact, like the athlete, you train for it, but you approach it with an intention of gaining or building a relationship for life. This is the most important relationship you will ever have, as everything else flows from and depends on it. Every other relationship and circumstance thereafter can fall into place, once you are in a right relationship with God. God is our source, God is our creator and we as created beings are part of him. Our relationship to him is our starting point, and he is our center point in our inner circle. He is our nucleus. Our lives have to evolve around him, otherwise we are off the radar. This is why nothing exterior can satisfy us: our longing is for wholeness which is only found in him. Where is he found? At our very center, our very heart, as God is in us and we in him. There is no separation from God, as the book *A Course in Miracles* tells us. This is very true, we are not separate from God, nor from each other. We are just extensions of his being, so by ignoring him we are in fact ignoring ourselves. When we neglect him, we are neglecting ourselves. We deny ourselves of our own very being, so it is no surprise that we are unhappy and spiritually void. We need and require God like we need oxygen to breathe and food for nutrition. We need to spiritually feed ourselves and nourish our inner being: our souls. By doing so, we are doing ourselves a great favor and justice, and our body and mind will thank us for that, because it is only then that we can feel complete, whole, and fully loved. By parenting ourselves we come to truly love ourselves; by attending to ourselves and by nurturing our inner hungers, only then do we fulfill our needs as human beings. This is of huge consequence to our general sense of self-worth and well-being; we find that we belong in this world and we are granted the comfort of feeling safe, secure, and loved. Only then when we love ourselves are we capable of fully loving another.

Self-love is by no means "selfish". It is a gift to oneself and to others. It is our very basis; without it we cannot build a proper foundation. As we get older and as our own parents pass away, as people hurt us and as life hardens us, it is essential that we do become a loving "parent" to ourselves. We need to "mother" ourselves and "father" ourselves throughout life. Most importantly, we need to be kind to ourselves. We need to take responsibility for our own inner happiness, to become spiritually mature, and in doing so we become more solid and self-sufficient. We are built up from within and not pulled down from without. What we become is not reliant on anything or anyone from outside; only that which is within will truly satisfy us. It is only then when our very basic needs are furnished that we can relax and concentrate on going deeper and deeper into our very essence, into our consciousness, where we can further discover the fruits of God and allow him to flourish within us.

To look after yourself in mind, body, and soul—i.e., to put time into your spiritual needs—is an investment for yourself into yourself, which will repay you in insurmountable ways and means. It is in no way a waste of time, as to come to know ourselves and to know God is what time is actually for. Spend your time in meaningful ways. Do not waste the precious time that we have on this earth. Our lives pass us by in the blink of an eye. Love is all there is, and as long as we grow in love of self, of God, and of others we will begin or continue to see the many blessings that life holds for us. We start to see reality through a more compassionate frame. When we truly love, then we become more open as people, and we develop and grow as God intended. By remaining in him and holding tight to him, we then can more easily see through the illusions that this material life can hold. Therefore that life becomes less relevant for us; our leanings are more toward Spirit and we are less occupied with triviality. We realize that there is so much more to life than the preoccupations of this world, that there is another world that is also around us and has a lot more to offer. That other world can help us face the challenges of this world with a renewed and different outlook. In fact, we realize we were never alone, that God was always there with us, only we did not realize it. By becoming aware of God and Spirit we can tap into a world of multiple possibilities. It is only by searching that we find, for if we do nothing, we find very little and we remain empty vessels. We are lucky to live in an age when we are educated and have easy access to books, learning, and the Internet. All resources are of great aid to reach wholeness and divine union. Yet it is not totally necessary to go to anything external for help either, as a genuine willingness to become closer to God is all that is needed. The seed has to be there before anything can be sown. Water your internal seed daily, feeding it nourishing things from reliable and good resources. Feed yourself very well on every level, be that physical, emotional, or spiritual. Pay attention to what you are allowing into your life—what you watch on TV, what you read, and what you listen to all have an effect on your quality of life and on your thinking. Trust in yourself, too; trust that you are worthy of divine union; we all are divine beings and have the same capacity. The difference is our choice to use it or not.

You can choose to meditate until you levitate off the ground, or you can watch TV; this is up to you. It is why God gave us free will. We are free to do as we choose. We can put ourselves on a good path, or we can continue on the road as we are. As is, we can live and die the same with or without God, so what is the difference? Why bother? We are going to die one day anyhow. "I can take my luck as it comes," you say. The difference is that a life lived in God will be easier, more fulfilling, and harmoniously better, and a life lived without is more empty. When you live your life in God's presence—which is right inside you—you automatically feel an interior peace. Nourish this, and it has a ripple effect that flows outward from you and into your life. Basically, you need to ride that wave with no life jacket on, as God's universe holds you up. Never be afraid to enter God's waters, as it is here where you will find your life's thirst quenched. Being close to God gives you courage for whatever comes in life, and you start to see that within each happening there is a blessing. You begin to notice the divine order all around you. It is there for you to tap into to make your life experience better. As I said before, God is here; he is real and very practical. God is useful, and he desires that we use him. That is why he desires our attentions; in order to help us have an easier human experience. He has given us many teachers, guides, and wise ones to enable us to help ourselves. He left us in an abundant universe with plenty to go around for all of us. He gave the universe natural laws by which it operates perfectly from. He offers us the same opportunity. We too operate with a system of natural laws that are here to assist us. Shelves are now filled with books discussing the laws of attraction, and how the universe can help us. All of this is true, all is there to aid us and all is given by God—if only we open our eyes and would use it. Jesus knew it too; he preached it in his commandment of love. Like attracts like and therefore love attracts love. Giving love fills our universe with goodness. Our consciousness is better equipped today to fully understand Jesus's teachings. Jesus taught in a manner that reflected the first century mindset; therefore, he taught in parables which reflect and mirror the human condition and God's love. All of life depends on love, for "God is love" (John 1:4–8), and we have God in us. Without love there is no point to life. But we cannot love the God within ourselves until we come to fully love and appreciate ourselves as we are. We concoct delusions about and around ourselves, so much so that we cannot see the Truth about life. Truth can be defined as spiritual awareness, or simply love.

We need to be kind to ourselves and to remember that we are God's perfect creation, as unfortunately the self-created delusions can damage us and those around us beyond repair. Allowing God into our lives can and will counteract delusions, if we are only open and receptive to him. Letting God enter our lives gives way for us to evolve and to grow, otherwise thorns entwine us, and their sharpness takes the sweetness out of life and out of us. This leaves us very wounded, and the deeper we are wounded the longer it takes for us to heal. Deeper wounds mean more deeply engraved injuries into our souls, our memories, and hearts. Past hurts and pains are not healed but amplified to exhaust our kindness to ourselves and others. We see mostly only the darkness and not much light. God lifts us to see the light once more, but you have to let God in first. You have to make first contact—this is why he gave us free will. God does not interfere with us, but leaves it up to us to acknowledge him or to ask for help. But we need to do both. First, we need to acknowledge him by praising him, giving thanks to him, living gratefully, and being aware of his presence in the universe and in us. Second, we have to ask him for help—ask and you shall receive (Matt 7:7). God cannot and will not interfere with our free will, so we have to ask him, ask his angels, his saints, his Holy Spirit, his teachers to help us. He gives us plenty of support, but sadly we do not tap into those resources or those gentle guides that can really help us. Too many cannot see. They do not want to see or even think about spirituality, God, and what happens after we die. They live for this world and this world only. This is convenient, of course—there are not enough hours in the day as it is, not to mention taking even more precious time and energy to think or to read about something, or to listen to some airy fairy insignificant meanderings that people think will make no difference to their lives or their future. How wrong they are. If they only realized that a life lived with heaven's support and guidance is far more profitable than a lifetime of self-struggle. If people only valued and realized what is available to them here and now, freely given and in the comfort of their own homes, our world would be a far happier place.

Chapter 5

Thanks

One thing that I cannot tolerate is ingratitude, or select amnesia, as I also like to call it. People so readily forget what a free gift we have been given in our lives today, how the gift of life itself is a blessing, no matter which form it takes. People live their lives with a sense of lack and insufficiency rather than seeing what they have. The notion of "keeping up with the Jones's" has never been so rampant. The materialistic monster preys on children and on young adults, selling them things they do not need. Society is under pressure at every angle from commercial cruelty. One now has to produce the picture-perfect Christmas, birthday, and holiday. Every event is now a huge money spinner for commercial sales. Actually, it is not necessary to have to demonstrate our compulsive, competitive consumer society. We seem to never have enough of anything; clothes, food, the latest models of everything, what was okay for last year. If we do not have the most recent of everything, we cannot be seen. Upgrading is the norm. Standards that we set ourselves have reached new heights, but in the wrong direction. I could rephrase that and say that we have in fact reached new lows. The monster of materialism has engulfed the planet. The rich still get richer and the poor even poorer as more and more resources and money are used up to fund this material monster.

"We have to live more simply so that others can simply live," said Mahatma Gandhi (1869–1948). The more we waste on "things" that we actually do not need or value, the less money is left for actually saving, rather than borrowing it or using it for charity, for that matter. It is better to buy our teenagers more makeup or video games than to fill the charity box or to invest in good causes. Anyhow, some of those charity boxes are brought into the home via the church, and if people are no longer going to church, they no longer receive the likes of their charity box or information. Our own material greed and thoughtlessness turn us away from the hungry child or the urgent need for medicines in less well-off countries. Thousands of hectares are cultivated annually to grow vines and grains to produce alcohol; one can very easily imagine a better use for agricultural land which is not so counter-productive. I am sure people have a heart and do care, as people are innately very good, yet we waste so much that could go to better use. That is material waste, and an oversight that needs attending to on our part. The biggest ingratitude tends to be toward God, for he is the one who gives all. He gave us life, a place to live and an abundance of resources to live from. How great is that? Do we really stop to think about all that we have? The air that we breathe, the water that we drink, the heat from the sun, all of life's free gifts; where did they all come from except from God himself? For when he created our lovely planet, he filled it with all that we need and plenty to go around for all of us; there is no need for anyone on our planet to be hungry or be in need of any kind.

Gratitude teaches us to be less self-centered, to acknowledge all that we have and not to focus on what we do not have, or *seem* to not have. It is a respect to show gratitude and in doing so, we show our appreciation for all that we have in life and all that we will have. By being genuinely grateful receivers, we show that we are indeed worthy of all that we have been given, and therefore will be given more. Again, it is consistent with the laws of attraction, and of course like attracts like. But, our motives have to be right in order to work properly within God's laws. You cannot project a false attitude in consciousness out into the universe. The universe and God cannot be fooled. You cannot only give lip service to maximize the potential of universal laws; all intent has to be genuine and must come genuinely from the heart. Gratitude forms part of the natural flow of life, and it is essential to the rhythm of giving and receiving. Without gratitude our lives become locked, slowed down, and stagnant. Gratitude is a response to love shown and it is characteristic of a balanced love. This love demonstrates healthy traits, and therefore it is not one-sided. It forms part of the two-way street. The receiver recognizes the giver and gives thanks for what has been received. But when what has been freely given falls into the category of the habitual or is taken for granted, such as air, water, health, breath, sight, hearing, dancing, thinking, reading, writing, hot water, food, love, loved ones, pets, joy, beauty, nature, and lots more, we tend to overlook or forget to simply give thanks for. Yet, without these we simply could not survive. By showing gratitude, directly or indirectly we are showing respect to not only the giver, but also to ourselves. Again, this is closely linked to the self-love that I speak about, without which nothing is possible. When we love ourselves we respect ourselves and we realize the value to what we have been given that is in ourselves, in our very own essence and being. You come to the point where you give thanks for what and who you are because after years of being lost, you are found, and what you have found, you actually like. This you appreciate and give thanks to God for. You fully realize your self-worth for the first time; at last you realize who you are and what you're capable of, all due to your connectivity with our Source, which is God. You realize that it is the good God who is the giver of all of life.

I personally had to nearly lose my life on a number of occasions before I fully and truly understood that. But I suggest the easier, far less dramatic option of just simple self-realization, introspection, and awareness. Extremes are not always necessary, yet many transformations have occurred due to life-changing dramatic ordeals such as illness, addictions, and extreme loss (such as victims of war who lose their homes, livelihoods, loved ones, and jobs; they are essentially left with nothing). Extreme wakeup calls have made people sit up and realize what life is actually really about, thus enabling their egocentric selves to be sidestepped, so that their True-Selves could finally shine through. And with this reawakening, there comes an immense sense of gratitude for seeing life as it should be, for seeing and realizing the gift that life itself really is. Your True Self is the divine being who you were born as; as opposed to your false self which is buried in egocentric behaviors, it is your insecurity, your fear manifesting into your everyday life. It is not remembering who your source is—essentially it arises and develops out of being separate from God. Having forgotten God, your fears and insecurities foster and take root, sticking you to the ground where you can't fly and be free to be who you really are and to realize all your dreams. But, if we remember God and remember that we owe him our grateful thanks for our lives and all the good we have, our darkness can start to lift. We begin to see all that we have, as opposed to what we don't have. We have many ways in which we can show our gratitude to God.

We can simply say thanks everyday for our lives, we can make gratitude lists to remind ourselves of all that we have, we can pray, or we can give back a little each day as a way of saying thank you to God. It is very important to do this, as you know; you can continually give to someone whom you love—your kids, yours friends, your family, whoever comes to mind—but if you get nothing in return (no affection, no thank you, no appreciation shown), how do you feel? Do you feel overjoyed and loved? No, you do not. Will you continue to give graciously to these people? Perhaps yes. But what will you bestow on the one who showers you with kisses, love, and affection daily without your asking? You can bet your boots you will give that person the best of your attention, your affections, and all your utmost love in return. I hope you have got the idea. It is not rocket science, but simple common sense that can transform your life and your relationship with God. Go for it, do it, live it, and become the person you were born to be. Be the very best edition of yourself. Do not settle for anything less, as God created us to create and build fulfilled lives, not half empty, half lived lives, but lives lived to the full, and lives lived in gratitude for the life we have been given.

Not every day of our lives is going to be lived in perfect bliss; there are always humps and bumps along the roadways of life, yet without them we would not learn much, or appreciate when we do have it good. Both good and bad experiences as we classify them are actually good. All is good, all teaches us and brings us into being and shapes our character. For me it is like a roller coaster— you cannot experience the thrills and joys without going up and down, round and round. All is made so we can experience to the max our earthly lives; we need to give thanks for this also, as every cloud does have a silver lining and as the old proverb goes, "when one door closes, another one opens." How true, even if we do not realize it at the time. But to fully appreciate this we do need to be self-aware and able to stand back and observe life objectively. This comes with time and from God, as we curl up closer and get closer to him, he helps us to see more clearly. God gives us clearer vision with which to see. Without God—without a relationship with him and awareness of ourselves—this is impossible.

We need to encounter God personally; when I say "encounter" I mean that you need to build a personal relationship with him. This is not found in textbooks, nor through learned behaviors, rites, or rituals. This is something completely different and even better, this is like having and enjoying a good friend by your side throughout your life. This is knowing that you are never alone, that you always have this entity with and in you. It is realizing that what you were searching for all along was right within you and always by your side. In fact, you are *never* alone. Spirit/God fills the empty spaces in and around us. Its awareness completes us. This is so comforting when you finally and fully understand that Spirit surrounds you at every moment of your life. That the end to struggling it alone is here for all of us to grasp. We have a life line and connectivity to heaven, twenty-four seven. We never have to struggle. We can call on heaven to help us at any given time, as heaven watches over us constantly. Tapping into this resource is a great advantage and blessing to have and to realize. To appreciate this and to utilise this gives us a huge "leg up" on our ladder of life. Sadly, many do not bother to know or they do not fully understand what is freely available to them. They think that spirituality is a waste of time; how narrow a presumption to make. How often do people lack and linger in misery when it is not necessary. If only people would give God a proper chance to enter into their lives. There are no losers here, only sadly wasted opportunities to really live life to the maximum. By being in constant and continual conversation with God, we spend our time in a worthwhile manner. We expand, "Truth" is learned, and spiritually we grow. From being in divine contact, or being connected to God, we consequently become more compassionate and loving people. Essentially we are tuning ourselves into heaven's airwaves, and this is a good station to listen to. It comes highly recommended, because when you are tuned in and aware, you never want to unplug that vital connection that is life-giving and good. This is what happens during meditation; you essentially tune into the universal channel of God's intelligence. This then enables that energy to enter into your consciousness, and thus into your life. This is very simple and available to all of us. For that too we need to say "thanks," as our potential is only starting to be realized, as we enter a new age of conscious living: lives lived in awareness.

Chapter 6

Positive Thinking: Rethought

In recent times we see many books written about "positivity" and the power of positive thinking, and the power of the mind. All of this is connected and in conjunction with what Jesus essentially thought. What the ancients told us and what Jesus handed down to us from his Father in heaven is now being resuscitated and remodeled in popular psychology—but many times without God, telling us exactly the same thing but in a different manner. Basic Christian teaching is centered on love—love of God and love of neighbor. Jesus was *the* hippie of his day, going around preaching "love." He essentially turned the old way of thinking on its head, teaching to no longer practice "an eye for an eye" as in the Hebrew scripture, but to "love" one's enemies instead. How positive was that? All of Christian teaching would fall apart without those elements of loving positivity; Christ embodied love, taught love, and gave love unconditionally. Jesus's life and death is the perfect example of love. Jesus, one could say, defined love and positivity itself, not only in his teachings, but more so by and with his actions. This guy practiced what he preached; he did not just give lip service or donations. He displayed enormous and unyielding courage. It is why I like and admire him so much. I also like the simplicity of his message—it's not complicated and it's easy to understand.

The hard part is putting Christianity into authentic practice. But, like all the recent contemporary body/mind/Spirit or psychology books, essentially what Jesus taught was positive thinking. Love for love itself takes on the dimensions of all that is good, all that is positive; it turns darkness into light, and continues into what we now call a "Christ Consciousness," that transforms our thinking and our universe. Both contemporary psychology and Christianity can say the same thing, but in a different manner. They are both paths to the same destination: a happier and better you. If you marry the two—both authentic Christianity and popular psychology—you have a marriage literally made in heaven. Christ was one of the greatest psychologists of all time. He knew and loved the human condition very well indeed. His parables alone demonstrate his ability and his insight into the human psyche. But most importantly, what Christ had was God. As God cannot be found in psychology alone, yet both religion and psychology are closely interlinked, so we need to understand ourselves in order to grow and transform. We are, after all, also rational beings. Our interior lives depend on our ability to introspect, to discern, to develop. St. Teresa of Avila is a perfect example of this marriage of mind and God. The Carmelite priest and writer John Welch recognized this in St. Teresa and drew comparisons between herself and the famous Swiss psychotherapist Carl Jung (1875–1961). Welch notes this in his introduction to his book *Spiritual Pilgrims: Carl Jung and St. Teresa of Avila*:

> "Both Carl Jung and Teresa of Avila were perceptive observers of human interiority. Teresa wrote about the soul, the human person in his or her relationship to God. Jung studied the psyche and the relationship of the person to his or her own depth. Each illumines our interiority but from a different perspective. Studying them together heightens their helpfulness."[1]

This is why there is now such a buzz surrounding Teresa of Avila and the resurfacing of the importance of meditation and

1. John Welch, *Spiritual Pilgrims: Carl Jung and Teresa of Avila* (New York: Paulist, 1982), 1.

49

contemplation as integral parts of our spiritual growth; because, quite simply, they are. Carl Jung, consequently, saw spirituality as the cure for alcoholism; he saw how it is only through spiritual transformation that we can actually fully heal. Spirituality is but a mix of psychology and the sacred; it is impossible to separate the two.

> About that conversation with his alcoholic patient, Jung informs Bill Wilson that "I could not tell him every-thing . . . in those days I had to be exceedingly careful of what I said." Jung was concerned about his reputation and did not want to be misunderstood or misreported. In his letters, Jung reveals that at that time he did not feel comfortable saying the following to his patient: "His craving for alcohol was the equivalent of . . . the spiritual thirst of our being for wholeness expressed . . . as the union with God."[2]

The person to whom Jung is speaking is Bill Wilson (1895–1971), co-founder of Alcoholics Anonymous (an organization which helps people to recover from alcohol addiction). Its guiding prin-ciple is the twelve-step program, which at its heart is a spiritual program.

To find God and to meet God, you go within yourself. It is in the silence of meditation that we can encounter God. Jesus himself said that he and the father are one (John 10:30), how God is in him and he is in God. The same is true for us. We are all divine, and we all carry the same DNA. It is our divine heritage and our divine right to be able to call on heaven for help, to tune into heaven's frequency and connect to God. It is what it is there for, as it is who we really are; pure Spirit. As I said; we are never alone. Jesus knew this, Jesus thought this and he lived it. We just need to learn this for ourselves I suppose. It was like me—I could have been told the same thing a thousand times, but it was not until I finally realized it for myself and I tried it that life began to improve for me. Believe

2. *Insight Medical Publishing,* psychopathology.imedpub.com/carl-jung -and-alcoholics-anonymous-is-a-theistic-psychopathology-feaible.php?aid =8504.

that all things are possible, and not just possible—very possible, if you put your trust in God (a positive God, that is).

True personal power is having the ability to free yourself of the constrictions of this material world, and find your true self within. It is when you are centered in your true self, encompassing a body, mind, and soul balance, that fulfillment truly is found. It is comparable to a good wine or cheese; as it matures over time, so too will your spiritual growth, but the important thing is to start. Start paying attention to how you live your life. If you are not happy, then something needs to change. This has to be your priority. This is your life and we get no second chances. Grasp God, come to know him and keep a hold of him, as he is your source, nothing in this material world will fully sustain you as Spirit. Remember that God and only God is your source in this life and the next. This world will pass away but our Spirit is infinite. To connect with our soul, our Spirit—which is who we really are—is our objective; this is why we are here. Do not allow the troubles of this world get you down, turn inward to God, and return to your source; find that inner peace and calm that you seek. This requires you to become intimate with God and this is only something you yourself can do. Nobody can do it for you. Yes, it requires a smaller effort on your part, yet it has benefits beyond compare. Anyhow, after having been given our lives freely; it is not a huge task to slow down and acknowledge the divine within us. It is there that we find God. It is there that we find comfort and consolation. It is in our interiority that we come to realize our spiritual heritage and realize that this material world really is passing; that Spirit is the only thing that is actually real, not the other way around. We really have to recondition our thinking from the traditional way of looking at life.

As I said we need to tap into God's/Spirit's higher consciousness and a higher frequency, this happens when we stand still and listen in silence to our inner being. This inner being is our divine spark and will guide us throughout life, if we only allow it. But, we have to be still to connect with the level of our soul, as the outside world distracts us so much that we cannot hear it properly. This is what happens when we drift along through life disconnected and unhappy. By being aware of Spirit all around and in us we begin to see things in perspective and do not allow insignificant material things to annoy us so much. When we realize that this life is only an illusion, and that only Spirit matters, and that this same Spirit is love, we therefore can quickly calm down and not get caught up in worrisome details, only focusing on what is important. We worry over the most insignificant of things, when all that really matters in the end is love. As God is love, it is he who matters and nothing else. When we die will we worry about the electricity bill, or how much we weighed last summer? Worry weighs us down unnecessarily and consumes our positive energies, sucking the life out of us. What will matter in the end is how much we loved and cared about each other during our lives. God knows we have material needs on this earth; I am not denying that we have bills to pay and children to educate. Yet God gives us help with all of life, so that we can better focus on the things that do really count, such as spiritual growth, loving ourselves, each other, and all of creation. God as our source gives us help with all, if we only seek it. By allowing ourselves time with God we find life's solutions. By bathing in God's goodness and love we too find peace, harmony, and the love we need and yearn for. All the love that we need is in us, given by God; we just have not unearthed much of it so far. But it is there and it is in endless supply. Each of us is a well of God's love, and with God as its source it can never run dry.

Having spiritual knowledge and awareness is a huge benefit in life. It is very a practical tool to equip you for life's ups and downs. It is only within the last fifty years via education and access to media sources that we as Christians have really begun to develop and explore our spirituality for ourselves. We recognize now or acknowledge our spiritual capacity, and this capacity is endless. Religion introduces us to God in a formal inherited manner, while spirituality is where we really meet him in personal experience. The trick is to not stay in this formal relationship, but to develop it into a more mature and beautiful friendship. We have a lot of avenues to explore these days with the Internet giving us many options; bookshelves are filled with sources on spirituality and well-being. All avenues seem to be open to us. Meditation is taking off as the new cool thing to do, evening classes in "mindfulness" are full. All this is positive and necessary to bring about a higher level of consciousness and spiritual awareness into society. Many know this new consciousness and awareness exits, but are people fully incorporating it into their lives? Or are people still running around like headless chickens? It is all very good in theory but needs to be practiced in a real and practical way. So how do we do it all? How with our busy modern lives do we fit it all in without being exhausted? We can fit God into our daily lives very easily; it can be done anywhere, anytime. The issue is to make a conscious effort and to stick with that effort no matter how small it may seem. We need to stop making excuses and we need to motivate ourselves and realize that this lack of spirituality in our lives is really a draw back. It is what is actually holding us back in life, and not what we think it is.

We grow and learn step by step, not by jumping in at the deep end. The process is almost comparable to changing our diet; it is the smaller things that produce lasting and effective results. Realistic goals are always more achievable and sustainable, as opposed to mega-martyrdom efforts, which only end in frustration anyhow. Finding peace and quiet to connect with God within you is not a luxury but a necessity; place it into your daily routine, as you do for brushing your teeth or walking the dog. And like brushing your teeth or walking the dog, when you go without for a day or two you feel like your mouth stinks, or you suffer from a lack of exercise and fresh air. It is amazing how without even realizing it, the stuff we can consider mundane or boring actually turns out to be the best thing for us. The daily choices that we make grow on us and make us into happier healthier people. Soon after it becomes a very healthy habit, but done "consciously" of course. This all has a ripple effect out into the greater world. If I am happier, then so too is my immediate circle, such as my family and friends; by making them happier they in turn pass it on into their outer circle. This ripple effect spreads out and out. Spirituality has the same effect—by being more balanced people we send out better vibes into our environment and beyond. These are not merely "vibes" but vibrations of the highest level from Spirit, for when we are in connection with Spirit we are at our peak. Our energy is good and we catapult this out into the universe. We do untold good by simply praying and releasing good energy into the atmosphere. We have huge capacity to impact on our planet at a subconscious level, yet we are not fully aware of this yet. Group consciousness has the power to uplift or to bring down whole societies. First the focus has to be on our own individual spiritual awareness and growth, and this has the domino effect as enlightened individuals go on to create enlightened societies.

Basically, we need our ego, but not to the extent to which it has developed into "me, myself and I." This is taking it too far. We do need our egos to drive the car and to function on a daily basis. We need to just drop the unnecessary egocentric and selfish behaviors; those that exhibit fear or a lack of love are the ones that need to fall away as a tree in autumn sheds its leaves. As we grow and mature throughout life, this realization should be, in theory, dawning on us. We should see the "light". As the tree with age deepens its roots into the solid ground, so too do we. We nurture and take root in a mature spirituality that will fulfill us and accompany us throughout life. It is interior—we can take this with us anywhere we go in the world. It weighs nothing and it costs nothing; low-cost airlines would be disappointed, and it is available twenty-four seven, so what more do you want? This idea that we are separate from God only widens the gap between the spiritual world and our material world. What I call "Spirit" or the "Spiritual world" is also "heaven," if you prefer to call it that. It is in any case the other realm that is invisible to our naked eye, and as stated, just because we cannot see it directly, does not mean that is does not exist. It is comparable to electricity; you know it is there—it powers the light bulb to come on—yet you cannot see the electricity with the naked eye. God and Spirit operate from the same principle. It is because God and Spirit vibrate at a higher level than us that we cannot see them. Electricity is the same; it too is nothing but energy, yet its vibrations are different than ours, so we cannot see it, nor is it solid like us. Everything in life vibrates at varying speeds; it is the only thing that differentiates us from other physical things such as furniture or trees. The slower the speed of vibrations the more solid a thing is to the naked eye. But as Spirit vibrates at a much higher frequency than us, we need to increase our vibrations to reach a spiritual level. Science is now catching up with religion, as what the ancients knew and practiced is now being realized and verbalized in science. This in itself is verification for the existence of varying levels of existence. We can exist but at varying levels; this is how death is conquered, as quite simply death does not exist. We merely change vibrational speed and carry on in the next world as pure Spirit.

But while we are still in this world, within this level of human existence, we all the more so need the connection to heaven and to Spirit to help and guide us through this life. This is our school and spiritual growth is our homework. We are meant to be evolving, growing, and learning to love as we move through this life. Love is the energy that fuels our inner light; this inner light is also God. Without this light we diminish and die. It is our most basic human essence; it is our divine DNA. People who are caught up in poverty, hunger, war, and destruction are denied this very basic right, as their basic needs are turned into a daily struggle for survival. They are consumed by life's devastating diversions; their focus cannot then be on spiritual growth. Yet here we are in the west with an abundance of choices, and either we refuse to see the disease or we are so blinded that we cannot. This *disease* you can call spiritually sleepwalking through life, spiritual blindness, or just simply being ungrateful to the Creator who gives all and who keeps on giving. This disease or disconnection results in much misery and despair, ironically helping to create the global imbalance. Call the disease what you will, but the fact remains that this disease is very easily cured.

Becoming whole again after being dismembered is a happy release. You are effectively released from your own prison that you yourself—through no fault of your own—actually created. This is what is meant by "the Truth will set you free" (John 8:32). When Jesus came to "save" us, it was not from anything exterior. He came to show us the way and free us from *our very selves*. This is what he meant in his teachings. He did not come to "save" us from the "devil" or anything exterior. He came to draw for us an interior map to the heart. This map leads us to his sacred heart, where only love abides. He knew the way; this is why he choose to tell us that he was the way, the Truth, and the life (John 14:6). Jesus showed us the way to wholeness; this wholeness is found within yourself; love of God, neighbor and self is the key. His way was inclusive and excluded nobody. He extended his love and compassion to all, and he knew full well that it is kindness and compassion that heal, and not harsh judgements. Jesus recognized how we are all one, and stressed that we truly need to love one another. Jesus was the ultimate guru of first century Israel. Jesus showed us how to live fulfilled lives, lives lived in companionship with God. His example was a life that is not distant from God but includes him, because to exclude God is to exclude ourselves; we effectively stunt our own growth, which is never a good idea.

By omitting God, we only damage our inner temple. We are not honoring ourselves nor our true identity. We are void inside. It makes sense really, and it is way cheaper than Botox. Because when you smile from the inside—illuminated in divine light, you literally shine. Your vibrational energies are lifted within you, so you radiate more joy, more positivity, and more love. Your aura is bathed in something that money cannot buy. You feel fully alive, you feel your self-worth, you feel well and it shows. It is a tool for life that will never leave you. It helps you, it comforts you, and it nourishes you from your inner depths. Having grounded yourself in spiritual awareness, you have that reassurance and guidance that automatically comes with it. You have at your disposal all of God's creative intelligence and love to guide you. But you must listen. You must be still in order to hear your inner voice speak to you. You must ask for help. When you are correctly and maturely connected to God and Spirit, you are intuitively directed by your higher self. This means that you can come to trust your instincts and emotions; this inner voice is Spirit leading you, this does not happen overnight, but builds over time. It grows and fosters as you become more comfortable within yourself and within your relationship with

God. This allows self-acceptance and love to develop even further. It is, in fact, a very precious, wonderful, and loving time for yourself and your Creator. It builds spiritual intimacy, and instills in you a realization that truly you are never alone. It is quite beautiful. Spiritual awakening enhances your quality of life; bringing it more depth and more lawyers to be enjoyed. Life is no longer empty, shallow, or meaningless. Life shows itself as beauty personified in this earthly existence, and each challenge that presents itself is no longer a challenge but an opportunity to grow, to expand spiritually in the direction of who you were meant to be. We are therefore fulfilling our very own selves, and we will have come full circle as we rotate internally, spinning a better life for ourselves.

Chapter 7

Mode of Employment

What we want to achieve is to open each day with an awareness of God in our lives. We need to give thanks to him for everything. This can be the basic springboard into every new day lived in collaboration between God and ourselves. This partnership between God and I is the foundation and corner stone of my life and how I live my life. Without that, my world would fall apart. Not all at once, but bit-by-bit. So, as you build your very own foundations with God, so too will your world improve; again not all at once, or even overnight, but step-by-step. As you raise your awareness toward God and heaven, your thoughts are connected and tapping into all that is good in the higher realms, creating peace and harmony within you; this in turn will be what you give out, and what you give out returns to you. This is universal law: what you put out comes back. It is the same as the "what goes around comes around" scenario.

This is key to our future as humans: as our consciousness expands, so too will our relationship with God. It will allow the grandiose of God in, so you can radiate that glory outward. By being connected into love's frequency on the higher vibrations of "heaven FM," you are now creating for yourself a life bound in higher consciousness. This is of the utmost importance for you as an individual and as a group consciousness; this can even prevent wars, as group consciousness is powerful and can create beauty or destruction depending on the thinking of the general masses. Fear has the capacity to turn negative thoughts into negative actions, and vice versa; loving thoughts has the same effect, creating actions of love. Thoughts are things and we need to anchor our thinking in love and positive emotions for us and for the world to profit. God gave us the solution to all our earthly problems, but unfortunately fear keeps this at bay. By building our foundations within God and love, we are starting to create that better world; this is very beautiful, very doable, and very easily achieved.

"The greatest thing anyone can do for God or for man is pray" said S. D. Gordan (1859–1936).[1] By simple prayer and by meditating in silence we can come to experience God. This is worked into our daily routine, so that becomes second nature to us, and we feel out of sorts when we neglect it. We can learn to grow in our love of God, to be in love with him, as we see and feel the fruits of spiritual presence at work in our lives. This presence may not be fully obvious to you until you learn to recognize and see with the Creator's eyes. This ability comes in time with spiritual growth. Call it God's grace if you like, but I see the ability to recognize the divine at play in the world, not so much as a "grace" given to only a chosen few, but as an ability to connect and tap into heaven's higher consciousness that is there for all of us. God does not hoard up his spiritual knowledge for only a chosen few; this knowledge, grace, or awareness is there for all of us, freely given as any generous loving Creator would do. You most definitely do not have to be the spiritually-elite to have capacity to experience God. But you do have to put in *some* time and effort, as like all worthwhile things in life; we have to put in a bit of ourselves. It is like going on holiday to that exotic beach you always dreamed of: first you wish to go, you start to save, you reserve, you start your weekly or monthly payments and you wait for time to pass. Next you travel to the airport, then you board the flight and you disembark at the other end. You take a transfer, and finally you arrive at your lovely beach.

1. S. D. Gordan, *Quiet Talks on Prayer* (New York: Fleming H. Revell Company, 1904), 2.

A sequence of events has to occur before you arrive at your chosen destination, and God and the spiritual path are the same. Like a lot in life, you do not just arrive without taking a journey that requires organization, time, and effort. Put in a bit of effort and your whole life's journey will be made a lot easier as you realize that you are not randomly journeying alone. You realize that this existence is most certainly not your final destination, nor your real life. This "bit of effort" can and will be enjoyable as you venture into a new phase of your life, which will now have more meaning. You start to go with the flow of the universe and not against it. You find your rhythm and your place in this universe. All of life has its rhythm and is organized in a specific manner. It is not some random accident that your heart beats without you telling it to. There is an intelligence at work in the universe; God is that intelligence and when you are connected to him you have the benefit of having that intelligence at your disposal. God's creative intelligence is in you, and you just have to access it. But sadly, spirituality today usually takes a back seat, which is ironic considering God's desire to drive us toward him and toward that better, easier life that I spoke of.

People have told me how great I was to have changed my life and turned myself around. But I was not by any means "great". What is marvelous is that I was given a great opportunity and I took it. Once I started the ball rolling in the right direction, life turned around for me. It was not by chance that I have come to where I am, but by my own design. I asked God for help and he gave it. Any good opportunity that I had to grow spiritually, physically, or mentally, I took it. In essence I responded to what life had to offer me. I lost any fear I had, I trusted myself and God, and I went for it. I had no huge commitments, only to honor the new life I was given, living it as best I could, and that I do. It has paid off for me. I gave myself the time that I needed to become whole again. It took a few years, of course, and life is a work in progress, but I spent and invested my time in myself wisely. Financially I sold what I needed to support myself and I dived straight into a new life. I read, I prayed, I meditated, and I ran. I exposed myself to nature, where her healing powers cleansed and comforted me. I did all of this without any guilt, without beating myself up about my past. I forgave myself, as I knew I had nothing to forgive. After all, I had only been an innocent lost child. Self-care is never selfish, but always a necessary investment, because if you are not well, you cannot look after yourself or the others who also need and depend on you. Nor does it matter what age you on are on paper; what manners is your rationality, your willingness to see life for what it really is, and your willingness to change. Hitting rock bottom broke my bubble and woke me up. It happens to different people at different stages of their lives, but realizations or awakenings thankfully do arrive. This is where you really start to live. I suppose that is why they say life begins at forty, as in theory you are wiser and more experienced. But that said, there are people who never got it, will never get it, and do not want to get it. Therefore, be very thankful for your intellect and eagerness to learn. Never take anything for granted. You have to be open to change, to learning new things and new ways of being. You need to stand with your arms wide open, ready to receive all that this life and this universe has to offer. You need to be "receptive" and "responsive"; both of these attributes are vital, because without action, nothing will actually happen. It is all well and good to have every cook book ever written, but without a meal on the table, your bookshelves may as well be empty.

What I have found is that to those who have, more will be given. Once you start the spiritual search and the longing takes over you to deepen your spiritual awareness, the doors flood open. It makes sense, as the more you seek, the more you find and the more fulfilled you become. It is a series of stepping stones leading down a path to your goal of enlightenment. Your consciousness starts to expand and allows for light to enter. This light is pure consciousness or pure awareness found within the light. Either way you are honing in on your True Self, or your soul. You start to live life from a different level, and life starts to exhibit more mystery and more richness than you ever expected. You begin to look at the world fresh and anew. You, in essence, can create a rebirth for yourself, a new beginning, one where you are at peace with yourself and the world around you. Being closer to our Source or to God—whichever you want to choose to call our Creator—makes you feel better, and this filters down into every area of your life and every cell in your body. You are more grounded and therefore calmer and more decisive. By listening in silence to the inner voice of your true self at your most intimate level, you gain confidence; uncertainty is no longer an issue, knowing that you are being guided by God's infinite intelligence. Worrying levels off as well, as you realize that there is no point, because that infinite intelligence that holds the universe is also holding you. You begin to totally trust in the process of life, and stress no longer has such a tight grip on you. Basically, you can relax knowing for sure that the universe with its divine intelligence is in control and knows what is best. It has done this for centuries and has lightyears of experience. How can you beat that?

It is important to realize that you are, in fact, pure Spirit, and that your body is not who you physically are—even though you co-exist, this does not make your body "you". Your body simply houses your Spirit as you journey through this life. You are your soul or Spirit, and when you start to live your life from this level, it is then that you find true happiness; this is because it is only then that you are completely whole. Once you start to feed your Spirit properly, life improves. It is that simple. Frankly, at present there are so many people who are hungry at the soul level; they are famished, yet they do not know what to eat. They gobble up life's garbage and digest it like it's good for them. They swallow what the mass media of TV, internet, and magazines tell them, such as what to buy, what to eat, what to wear, how to look, how to think, how to act, and how to live. It is why when Jesus said that whoever eats his flesh will live forever (John 6:54), he really was on to something. He knew then (and even more so today) that we are, in fact, hungry.

The five loaves and the fish of the gospel story was also a re-minder of how being fed at the level of Spirit produces miraculous results. Food fills a hungry gap; we need to fill ourselves up and fuel ourselves for life from the inside out. Our tanks cannot run on empty, and this is why I ran out of steam earlier in my life. I was not fueling myself at all. But once I started feeding my soul properly, everything else fell into place organically for me. And when this happens, you begin to exhibit qualities that Spirit represents and embodies and to mirror Spirit's fundamental Truth. You become a reflection of love at your highest level. You reflect God, so your actions are inspired, and your inner being is shaped by this new awareness. You may already be doing this without realizing it by living in an authentic awareness of who you really are in Spirit; if so, then you are living a justified life lived to its ultimate capacity. Anything less is keeping you in an unhappy state of existence. This is why it is so important to at least become aware of the benefits of spiritual awareness. It helps you to live your life to the max, where you were really born to be, and gives you the freedom and the courage to do just that. Therefore, your full potential is realized, because when you open up to God, that higher intelligence, all things become possible. Your life experience takes on another dimension; it can become an enjoyable one, lived in harmony, as balance enters your life. You are more centered and balanced from feeding yourself properly at the level of body, mind, and soul. Each level of your existence needs to be nurtured and looked after properly—otherwise, you are out of sync. Treat spiritual awareness seriously, almost like a subject to be learned and practiced. Educate yourself in the spiritual realm; do not remain in darkness when there is a lot of light out there to be found. This light will illuminate your way in life, as it is pure, divine, white light; awareness actually is light. Light signals hope, warmth, and purity. It banishes the darkness once you start to let that light in; again, this is where being open applies, because when there is no light nothing can live. Imagine the tunnel of the megalithic site of New Grange, County Meath in Ireland not being filled with light each winter solace on December twenty-first. Picture the damp, cold darkness never receiving the sun light. How miserable is that? Now again switch your attention back to the sunrise on December twenty-first, this time with sunlight filtering slowly down the tunnel to illuminate the entire chamber. The two images are not quite the same, are they? Imagine that the inner temple of your being as the same. You need that light to enter slowly and steadily to illuminate you from the inside out. You need to be filled with that divine white light, and that same light needs to be carried to every cell in your body.

Chapter 8

An Outdoor Orchestra

The light I spoke of carries within it God's divine intelligence, and it is this very same intelligence that raises the sun every morning and puts it to bed every evening. Divine intelligence surrounds us all the time, and this is most evident in nature. Nature is pure, loving, divine intelligence actualized; left to its own devices it lives perfectly, and yet has no brain. We on the other hand have brains and we cannot live as intelligently. This is why nature is so soothing and healing: it demonstrates to us perfectly God's loving divine intelligence at play without any ego getting in the way. God is just lovingly conducting his outdoor orchestra. But we can be guilty at times of taking nature for granted, as we have become so accustomed to it, or we are too far removed from nature in our cities. This is why we feel better when we are in nature, as it is there that you experience God more easily. Never underestimate the power of nature to restore, rebuild, and repair our wearied selves. Nature's natural pureness elevates us energetically and its freshness and cleanliness heals us; it also cleanses our chakras (our body's energy points). Anything that pollutes our planet, pollutes us; it affects our capacity to live and to connect with Spirit. Do not forget that we too are part of nature and of God's outdoor orchestra, we simply went indoors; but we are still all one in nature.

There is no separation between us and the natural world. Sadly, toxins interfere with our capabilities. These toxins from the environment, our homes, cosmetics, detergents, and foods, slowing us down mentally and physically. Eating pure, natural, organic foods and living a toxin-free life is vital for our overall well-being, and especially our spirituality. When your system is free—that is, when your body is not busy fighting off toxins and the like—then it is more available to you to connect with Spirit. You can hear your inner voice from within and your angels more easily and more clearly. You become like the tree in the forest, more organically in tune with the divine dance that is all around you. Our lifestyles have a detrimental effect on us at every level. Stress, of course, acts in the same manner; increased stress levels mean that the body is in a constant state of alert and therefore cannot function to the max on any level—be that physical, mental or spiritual. Reducing stress levels is vital to living happy, healthy, self-fulfilled lives. Stress can easily be controlled once you realize that you are, in fact, creating it yourself, allowing your mind and your ego to dominate and devour you. But again, being connected to God thankfully eliminates this.

Exercise naturally brings much-needed benefits to our bodies. It aides us both emotionally and physically. The benefits of physical exercise are well documented, but on a spiritual level you also benefit very much from physical exercise. Being physically fit you are also better able to hear your inner voice, as your blood circulates better and with less effort. You are lighter and more energetically balanced. Better still, if you are exercising outside in nature you are getting both the benefit of your exercise, plus that of being close to the healing and cleansing power that is found in nature. All these combine to free up our systems from lethargic lifestyles and toxins, allowing us the chance and opportunity to really live as God intended: in touch with ourselves, in touch with nature, and in touch with him, who is the Creator and Source of all. Mindless hours sitting in front of the TV watching rubbish does not feed our minds. I like the way Juice Master Jason Vale equates the TV with "Total Vegetable"; he could see the parallel between the two. In his book *The Juice Master: Turbo-charge Your Life in 14 Days*, he notes under the sub heading "Total Vegetable":

> Television hypnotizes us for hours on end; it sucks our energy and robs of us our precious time, time which we can never get back again. It's true that we like to "veg out" in front of the TV from time to time, but we don't want to veg out so much that we turn into one. Perhaps that's why the expression which describes someone who sits in front of the TV and doesn't move from the settee for hours includes a vegetable—potato of the couch kind, to be precise!"[1]

I agree, if you are watching rubbish and allowing your family to feed out of the same rubbish bin for hours. Placing children in front of violent movies and games does not help to rear peaceful, loving, and calm persons. Nobody wants their children to grow up to be aggressive, yet it is very convenient to place them for hours on end in front of a screen depicting violent images. This passive attitude is not a help for the next generation, who are so attuned to seeing violence and pornographic images that these things seem normal and standard. What we feed our eyes and our ears with is immensely important. How we spend our time is molding us and the world we are creating for ourselves and our loved ones. We need to be consciously aware of how we are spending that time, and how our children are spending their time. Our time needs to be spent wisely; we need to invest our time in creating and building a better quality of life. Do not waste time looking at senseless TV when you could be reading, cooking, painting, meditating, exercising, or learning a new skill. We only get one chance at this life, so let us make the best possible use of it. It is not rocket science, only common sense.

Stand back and look at life for a while. Live it in awareness of all. Become more aware of what is being sold to you by our consumer society, get off that commercial conveyor belt, and free yourself and your family. Concentrate on what really matters in life, like love. Love has the power to create this ideal heaven on

1. Jason Vale, *The Juice Master: Turbo-charge Your Life in 14 Days* (London: Thorsons, 2005), 73.

Earth. Heaven is here and now, so try to expand your vision of love, to see a wider horizon. Authentic self-love springs from the fact that you connect with your interior intimate Spirit, which is so pure that you cannot help but feel love. This purity radiates love, beaming it into every cell in your being; you just can't avoid it. Real self-love organically happens when you start on the road to enlightenment and union with God. It is pure love, and you feel this inside of you. You recognize it as coming from Source when you feel that love that is inside of you and it begins to radiate outward. This experience is available to all who take the time to seek their True-Selves, which is inside of all of us in the form of Spirit. This soul/Spirit or divine spark within comes from God. It is the part of us that lives on after death, our divine DNA—our umbilical cord attached to God, if you want to call it that. We all have one Spirit and we are all the same. Nobody is without. We just see life differently as individuals. But at the basic level of Spirit, we are all one and interconnected. This is why the "me, myself and I" theory never worked well, as it allows for holes and cracks to appear in society. It causes and creates division. "Wholeness" as a term has become very common in recent years. This term refers to us being complete as human beings in mind, body and soul, but it also refers to us a race. This wholeness needs to reflect our unity as human beings. Sadly, the fear of lack has historically pushed forward a "first come, first serve," very competitive society. This structure has not served all of society well and only created larger gaps between rich and poor.

Wholeness needs to encompass the "oneness" of all of mankind. We are all in this together. We are all experiencing life at the same time at this given moment in our history. But, we need to learn from our past histories and the generations that went before us. We need to realize that their lives were lived in context with their times, and that their times were very different from where we are today. We have been naturally evolving over the centuries and the level of consciousness has steadily grown. Our outlook and our thinking has expanded, and has outgrown past generations. That is not to say that we are "better" than what went before, however;

what I am implying is that a change has occurred. We have built this change on what went before, it snow-balled, and it continues to grow. This "change" I am referring to is a change in consciousness. Like I said earlier, society has become more compassionate, and we better understand ourselves now and this universe that we live in. Old fears and superstition no longer hang over us. Science has helped us to better understand things. The old feudal systems are gone, and people have more equality. More emphasis is being placed on authentic spirituality as opposed to hypocritical belief systems. Society has gone through major changes in recent years, mostly for the good and some for the not-so-good. But we do need to change some of the mentalities that we have inherited from past generations, such as fear of lack and this "me, myself and I" mentality. Not caring about our neighbor, only being fixated about our own existence; it only backfires. It always has and always will, until we really realize that by hurting my neighbor, I am hurting myself. But who is your neighbor anyhow? Who or what constitutes a neighbor? For me and my understanding, my neighbor is everyone, and every living thing. Yes, every living thing. What is bad for the mountains, the air, the birds, the oceans, the horses, the cattle, the stones, the trees, the children in Calcutta, the drug user in New York, the worker in Bangkok, the surfer in Los Angeles, my sisters, my next door neighbor, is also bad for me. Wholeness or oneness cares for, respects, and protects all that is on Earth. The term is not, never has been, and never will be exclusive to humans. Our vision of self needs to take on a new, expanded meaning. But, an expanded consciousness does just that; it is inclusive and does not exclude anything or anyone. Expanded consciousness will create a better world for us all, but like everything it takes time. It is happening, however; there are a number of very good teachers out there at the moment who are enhancing the way forward for people, showing that there is another, better way to live: a life lived in communion with creation, from the level of the true self. Because when you live from that level of your true self, you expand outward toward all of humanity and all of creation. You become in touch with all that is out there in our natural world and you resonate with it. You realize that you are not, in fact, separate from anything. You realize that you are part of God's orchestra; which is being played out perfectly on a daily basis, and you realize that the choir would be out of tune without you. You find your place in the world and you flow with the natural tune. You come to realize that you are in harmony with all. This may all sound airy fairy, yet it is very true and factual. Try it: give your soul the room to breathe. Work with it and see the effects for yourself. Your soul/Spirit, or your true self, is very practical and useful, so use it. It was given to us for a reason and that reason is because it *is* who we really are; therefore we can live better and happier lives. The masquerade ball we are all attending can end. If you can see past this life's illusions and live from this authentic level where all is seated, you will find your heaven on Earth right there inside of you. It is free of charge, of course. No admission fee is required. It is not an exclusive club, either; there are no restrictions here. Freedom is for everybody and is available to everybody who seeks for it from the inside out.

Chapter 9

A Tug of Love

The spiritual journey is unique for everybody. There are no set rules or patterns. It is an open-ended book, really, yet this book has the ability to guide your life experience. You are accompanied on your life's journey, so to speak. It is a great comfort and consolation to realize that you have this marvelous free gift available to you. Nobody can take it away, and you can bring it with you everywhere you go. You are a spiritual being having a human life experience, remember. Spiritual growth and awareness is taking responsibility for your own life and happiness. It stops one from aimlessly wandering through life, and gives life deeper meaning and purpose. It adds layers to the sponge cake we call life. It adds the double cream, instead of the simple single creamed version. It gives more taste and texture to life. It adds to the mystery and intrigue in this human experience we are having, opening up for us whole new worlds. Through prayer and silence in mediation, and by tapping into God's creative intelligence that is otherwise blocked out by daily hustle and bustle which we allow into our lives, we gain access to our deeper consciousness at the level of the soul. It is there, where we visualize and solidify our notion of true self: in Spirit. We see things that otherwise we would not. We meet ourselves in another form, one which is formless and free from all the garbage this material life throws at us. I know I have said the same before, but it is true. It is there where you find peace.

This peace is very important, as it grounds you and you come to know God better. The inner peace and glow of warmth that you find buried deep inside is of God, and it brings you closer to your Creator and Source. You can feel your internal love furnace burning away inside of you. This fire is never extinguished; it will burn on forever. By simply connecting with the universal creative loving intelligence that is our Source, we expand also into this consciousness that is God's. Our Creator and Source is available to us and anything that brings us into conscious contact with him has the ability to transform us, therefore making us happier and more complete. Without this contact we tend to drift more aimlessly through life, feeling a bit lost. We simply feel lost without our lifeline; we are disconnected and do not even realize it. We forget who we are, and we are tangled up in life's worldly web. To untangle and release ourselves, we need to rediscover ourselves a bit and loosen our inherited mindset, to adjust and grow into a new way of thinking and being. This new way involves living life more consciously, in the sense of living a life to the fullest, not ignoring any part of our being—that is, body, mind, and soul. It is the soul that should take our primary concerns, as everything follows from there. It produces a domino effect into every area of your life. Once you start living from the level of the soul, the rest falls naturally into place. For me, I had to come to an end point: rock bottom. This catapulted me into a new life and a new way of being, in which I lived from the level of my true self. I discovered that there is an another, better way to live and I liked it. I liked the new me and my new world vision that came with that. I got a new deal and a new package, and I took it with open arms.

I gave the process the time that it deserved. It has brought me immense personal pleasure and true power (a personal power as opposed to worldly power). I became stronger and more confident, as I learned to trust myself and what my soul was telling me—once I tuned in and listened, of course. This in time brought personal clarity for me, and a lot of my insecurities vanished. I think a lot was due to loving myself for who I really am for the first time in my life, and this allowed for an authentic relationship with my true identity, as opposed to what others thought I was, or who I wanted to be for others. Hitting rock bottom did me a lot of favors, even if the journey from wreck to wonderful wholeness was hard at times. I think the key to my newfound appreciation of life was that my essence had essentially totally burnt up and withered before, meaning that I really valued the refreshing waters given by my second chance at life. It resurrected me, reinflating my very being once again. It was like being given oxygen after years of suffocation. Yet, at the time of suffocating I did not realize how much I missed air until I actually got some. It was only then that I realized how much I had lacked and missed out on. It made me feel that I had a lot to make up for and give thanks for. I have a lot to be grateful for, really. But I have found that on the search for wholeness and especially spirituality, the more I sought, the more I was given. It is amazing how the universe gives back as soon as you start working with it, as opposed to going against it or (more correctly) against yourself. Movement occurs in your life, but in the right direction, like the book that you did not know you needed appears and helps further you along your path, enabling further personal growth. You are in harmony within this universe. All is possible and all is potential. Life flows for you as opposed to the tide being against you, and the interior internal tug of war one once endured can finally come to an end. My internal tug of war finally became a tug of love. Quite simply, I gave life a second chance, and it too supplied me with a second shot. It was the start of our collaboration, the two-way street that paved the way for my new life.

I give thanks in the manner of gratitude, including prayers of thanks to God and gratitude lists, and I give attention in the manner of meditation, prayer, reading, research, etc. In return, I receive my happy, expanded, larger life, centered in peace and harmony. It is that simple. It is an equation, nothing personal. I am not anyone special. I just try. It is how God designed the universe: organized and with laws that have a loving purpose. Examples include the natural laws like the laws of gravity, but also energetic laws of attraction, as in like attracts like, and "reap what you sow," as St. Paul put it in Gal 6:7–9 This biblical passage indicates that what you give out is what you will receive back. It is the basic law of attraction; like a magnet, like attracts like. But all of God's laws should amount to creative love. It is what he does best. And it was with this creative love that we too have been created, and we continue creating through our lives. But, we need to understand the universe in which we live; nothing in this universe is random. All is by intelligent design, and by following the natural flow of this universe, life flows easier for us—that is, if you work within God's laws. That is a must, and I repeat that the positive loving philosophy found in Christ's teaching demonstrates this wonderfully. Jesus shows us how to live better lives. His teachings of love, of God, and love of neighbor can catapult your life to new heights, if you consciously give it a try. There was meaning in the madness Jesus spoke about; it was not all happy, clappy, hippie babble. He understood the workings of God's universe, which has God's intelligent organization to it, such as what we can call science, which he put all into understandable human language for us. Jesus knew how the universe works, but remember that he had an audience of limited awareness, and only those who were open could try to follow him. Jesus got the concept of living an authentic life centered in love, as love given is echoed out into the universe and returned to you tenfold. Love creates more love on this our lovely planet and in our daily lives. It was Jesus who would demonstrate what it really means to love and to lose your false egocentric self, and he expressed this freely when he let them nail him to a cross on the side of a hill.

Chapter 10

Spiritual Footprints

Spiritual awareness need not be religious as in the sense of an organized religion. It is more intimate then that. Spiritual awareness means to be aware of the divine workings that are all around us. Spiritual growth can be a private process, and is unique for each of us as individuals as we all have our own unique road maps for life. But we are still all tied together as one spiritual family. As the universe operates in a non-biased fashion, this process is open to all of mankind. Transcendence is built into us naturally; we are all born with the divine spark within us. Being aware of who we really are, and tapping into all that is available to us, activates our inner power to heal ourselves and develop our level of consciousness. spirituality is neutral, and has the potential to create a new world order, where there are no religious wars or differences. What I am saying is that the commonality between all religions outweights the differences. Transcendence is the underlying commonality, the ability to transcend or go beyond this world through consciousness and encounter the next one, found right there inside of you. This is where God really is. He is not necessarily within a church, temple, or mosque, but inside of you. That said, religious sites do help you encounter God, of course.They are necessary places to come together to worship and praise God. Plus, they have the enormous benefit of being "power points," which possess higher energy levels and vibrations, enabling healing. Places that bring people together to pray have a higher energy field, as positive group prayer intentions hang within the atmosphere of these sacred places, adding to the positive spiritual presence already there. We should tap into that realm, that higher energy field, while in these holy places of worship. This you can do via prayer or meditation, which brings us into that higher energy field of existence.

Have you ever noticed how the presence of prayer transforms the atmosphere of a place? Everything is more calm, serene, and peaceful. This is because the prayers access the higher energy field where Spirit exists, with the added effect of uplifting the energy within that vicinity. It has been proven by quantum science that thoughts are energy, so that is how it is scientifically done.

> Your mind, your thoughts, your ego, the part of you that you typically think of as your "self" are all part of the quantum domain. These things have no solidity, and yet you know your-self and your thoughts to be real. Although it is easiest to think of the quantum domain in terms of mind, it encompasses much more. In fact, everything in the visible universe is a manifestation of the energy and information of the quantum domain. The material world is a subset of the quantum world. Another way of stating this is that everything in the physical domain is made up of information and energy. In Einstein's famous equation, $E=MC^2$, we learn that energy (E) equals mass (M) times the speed of light (C) squared. This tells us that matter (mass) and energy are the same thing only in different forms—energy equals mass . . . So the mind is a field of energy and information. Every idea is also energy and information.[1]

This is why Jesus said in Matt 18:20 that where two or three shall gather in his name that he will be there. Crowds work better because the group level of consciousness creates a much higher energy field and the strength of God's presence is therefore multiplied. It does not divide God, but creates a place where his presence

1. Chopra Deepak, *Synchrodestiny: Harnessing the Infinite Power of Coincidence to Create Miracles* (Great Britain: Clays Ltd., 2005), 36–43.

is amplified or reinforced. Group consciousness has enormous power to endorse and heal, and to expose God's creative, healing energy. If you ever get a chance to visit significant religious sites—or even smaller ones—take it. Tap into the higher energy that pulsates in that holy ground. If you ever have a choice between a week in Ibiza, Spain or a weekend in Jerusalem, I would practice my Israeli first. The high vibrational energy that is in Jerusalem is elevating, as it is a major pilgrimage site for the three Abrahamic religions; Judaism, Christianity, and Muslim. It is most definitely a major power point on the planet. It is the amount of prayers offered there that allows it this status. Even passing ten minutes in the atmosphere of a quiet, small church, has the potential to transform your mind and raise your spiritual vibrational levels, helping you feel better. Also, you take this energy away with you when you leave. It is like a peaceful spiritual shadow that will follow you. In addition, you bring your spiritual energy to the place you visit, adding to its already-accumulated energy; and leaving your much-needed spiritual footprint there for others to pick up on. Therefore, others who follow your visit benefit from your presence. Without realizing it, people give the gift of each other. We are all interconnected in many ways that we do not realize.

Spirituality aims to enrich people's lives by bringing about more loving, compassionate people who are open to purifying their egocentricity and redirecting their lives toward a higher reality that is centered in Spirit. Spiritual awareness paves the way for an inner path which enables people to discover their own essence. This is very important for western Christians where dogma, rites, and ritual have historically been at the foreground. We need to take the time to examine ourselves, to take ourselves seriously as spiritual beings. We need to recover our original form, which came from God. Spiritual growth is a process of inner transformation, be it grounded in a specific religion or not. Regardless, what is required is that it is authentically done. It requires both spiritual and psychological growth. I keep within the Christian context because for me not only is Christianity God-centered, but Jesus Christ was one of the best teachers and the psychologists of them all; he knew the human condition very well, and we can learn so much from him and those who authentically followed him. Life requires balance, and it must be lived within an authentic self-presence. Being too busy or trying to find happiness from the outside in, does not work. It is only when we are happy from the inside out that life actually works well for us. Being rooted and connected to God and to home fulfills our goal of happiness perfectly.

Spirituality is simply connection to Spirit, and this cannot be found in popular psychology alone. Yes, self-help books are a great resource, but often they lack God and Spirit. This is the vital link in the chain of life. No God is no good. We need this vital link, as it is our pulse, and without it we are spiritually dead. I know, as I found that out the hard way. It was not until I rediscovered my divine identity that I found my true happiness. Once I woke up and realized that God/Spirit/Source was available to me, I never looked back. I used what was available to me to build a better life for myself, my family, and society at large, because by being connected to Spirit, by living a balanced life, I made life better not only for myself but for others too. I am now whole and able to contribute to society rather than just cause problems for everybody. The love that I found was not exclusively for me, myself,and I. It was not a self-promoting or self-serving love; but an expanding love, that engulfs all who one comes into contact with. I can now contribute to this world by leaving a spiritual footprint, whereas before I staggered and stumbled along. Thankfully, the turmoil and chaos are gone, and the inner happiness, peace, and calm I was longing for all along has replaced them.

Chapter 11

Renewed Reviewed Energy

H aving been placed within a universe that is ordered and organized has many underlying benefits that we do not always realize. The fact that we now know life is operating energetically, both at a physical and a metaphysical level, allows us to better understand how our bodies and how our energy fields really work. Energy-healing work, such as Reiki and acupuncture, no longer seems so mysterious as science catches up with practices that have been used for centuries. Better understanding and more knowledge help us to comprehend the workings and mechanism of our bodies and our environs. Given that we are individuals, each a body mass of particles of energy, it comes as no surprise that we are affected by the various energies we come into contact with. Life as seen from the point of view of our metaphysical energetic bodies—that is, our aura on the outside and our internal energy flow on the inside—are constantly toiling to remain clean, and to be balanced at all times. Most people do not operate at their maximum energetic levels due to not being remotely aware of the existence of their sensitive energy fields. Energy is all around us and in us.

This energy needs to be attended to; otherwise, it slows us down, and we feel ill and lethargic. When I say "attended" to, I mean we need to learn how to look after ourselves; i.e., our energy fields. Our emotions and our environs affect our energy.

Imbalances from emotional stress, negativity in thoughts and action, transferal of negative energies from person to person—all can accumulate to hinder our energetic and spiritual selves. We need cleansing and healing inside and out to keep our energy clean, cleared, and balanced. The primary place to start is in our thinking, in our minds and our hearts. Positive thoughts create positive energy, and negative thoughts create negative energy. Loving thoughts, being positive, create positive energy, and therefore put positive energy out into ourselves and the world at large. In contrast, bad thoughts and bad behaviors put out lower, negative energies into our world, contaminating it. We have a duty not to only ourselves, but also to others to correct this and to try our best to put only good energy out into our lovely world. We are physical beings, and our thoughts are energy; any negative energy that we create we can potentially clear ourselves. But the cleansing of our hearts, minds, and behaviors are of primary importance. Carrying emotional negativity, if not dissolved, will manifest as illness, addiction, or depression during one's lifetime. As a result, our energy flow is blocked. This is when and where problems start to arise. Emotional issues need to be attended to and not buried or carried in the form of guilt, anger, resentments, bitterness, and so forth. Emotional baggage wears you down, and your energy literally draws from your body's energy, which clogs up your natural energetic flow. Energy forms clumps, which create bumps and lumps, knots of tension, as in stress knots in your back, neck, and shoulders. These are easily identified and felt, but the interior lumps and bumps that we cannot see go on to create cancers and the like. This is why energy is so important for us to understand, to get the connection between emotional well-being, energy, and our health.

Our bodies are a reflection of our state of mental health, of our inner well-being. We have to attend to ourselves and take energy seriously, because our state of mind affects our health, and our health is managed by our body's energy flow. It is a domino effect, one setting off the other. Energy also becomes clogged and slowed down due to our environs, such as contact with negativity, lack of exercise, of nature, of fresh organic food, and fresh clean air. Basically how and where we live affects our body's energy field. But as luck would have it there are age-old remedies for evacuating negativity from your environs and your body, and these work well—in accordance with having a loving heart, of course. Salt, especially sea salt, has an excellent cleansing effect; bathing in sea salt cleanses your energy field, as does the burning of dried silver-leaf sage. Lavender counteracts negativity too, and if you research the Internet you will find lots of information on how to counteract negative energy from yourself and your environment. Practical efforts in accordance with being loving and emotionally balanced help decontaminate our environs and our body. Other ways to decontaminate include Reiki or other chakra cleansing/balancing practices and massage sessions—these all stimulate correct energy flow within the body, and they help to maintain a better state of being for us. The better our energy flow is, the better and more available are we to connect to Spirit and to ourselves, as our inner divine spark, our essence, our soul/Spirit is contained within our physical body.

Our bodies are vessels for our Spirit. Remember, in essence we are but pure Spirit; we are not our bodies, as our bodies will pass away but our Spirit will live on. Therefore, the purer our energy is, the closer we can come to Spirit. Plus we feel healthier and have more energy to concentrate on what really matters in life; our time and energy are not wasted, and ultimately our quality of life is better. That's what we are aiming for, after all—to live the best life that we are capable of. The notion of mind, body, and soul is inseparable, as all three have to be lived in harmony and in balance. Otherwise, we are not whole. You take away one piece of the jigsaw puzzle and it cannot make the full picture. We need all pieces to be complete. That is why I make the effort to exercise, meditate, pray, burn incense, and candles as the light banishes the darkness of negativity and is a symbol of hope. I rub lavender on the soles of my feet and make gratitude lists daily, every week I take salt baths and burn sage, and I work hard to eat healthy. All of this is a help to keep me in spiritual, mental, and physical shape. Since discovering the importance of energy, and since I began consciously cleansing my energy field both inside and out, I can now tell if I am carrying negative energy, and I can feel it the moment I walk into an area where there is a lot of negative energy. To feel bad energy is almost like a wave of toxic waste washing all over your body; the more you cleanse yourself, the more sensitive you become to energy's influence. But this is a positive advantage; the fact that you are more aware of the varying energies around you, the more you will recognize and realize where positivity and negativity lie, and you can do more about it. Basically, it puts the ball in your court. This is a huge asset to have, and like everything worth having, this sensitivity to energy comes over time. If you are not already cleansing yourself, your home, your office, and your car, I recommend you start; and remember, just because a thing cannot be seen, it does not mean that it does not exist. Ask any scientist if you don't believe me. It was like meditation for me until I tried it and gave it the proper time and attention that it deserved, and only then did I start to reap the rewards.

This is what it takes to have anything worth having: a little bit of effort, patience, openness, and of course, taking the time. Not having the "time" to meditate, to pray, or to cleanse is not an excuse, and if you recognize yourself here, then you are the person who really needs to meditate, pray, and basically slow down. When I talk about "openness," I mean a willingness to be open to learning new things about yourself and this universe. If you start off with a very narrow vision, it is going to be harder to widen your horizon. Your sunrise will be only half of what it is capable of—it won't allow enough light in. Again, it would be like Newgrange on a very overcast December twenty-first. No sunbeam would magnificently bounce off the back wall to illuminate all. Your mind is the same; it needs that illumination. You do need to be open-minded if you want to fully explore and exploit your spiritual potential. Being closed can possibly counteract your progress and hinder your advancement. Basically, I found that by letting go and letting God show me the way, by asking for directions and giving in to him, by falling backwards into him and into the process of evolving, I actually grew. I went with the flow and the process. I didn't fight it, nor was I frightened by it. Once I saw life for what it really is, I started to move on and build something better. I took every opportunity that presented itself to me and I never looked back. My focus was on what was straight ahead and never behind; what had been my chaotic past was just that: past. I wish nothing but the same, and much love for you on your journey of discovery.